Augustinian Novitiate
Racine   WI,
53402

WAYS OF PRAYER SERIES
Basil Pennington, OCSO
Consulting Editor

Volume 12

# Can We Still Call God "Father"?

## A Woman Looks at the Lord's Prayer Today

*Céline Mangan, O.P.*

Michael Glazier, Inc.
Wilmington, Delaware

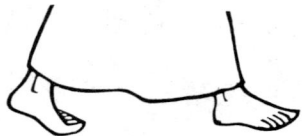

## ABOUT THE AUTHOR

Céline Mangan, O.P., is a graduate of the University College, Dublin, and the Pontifical Biblical Commission, Rome. She currently teaches in the Semitic Department, University College, Dublin. Her publications include *I Am with You — Biblical Experiences of God*; and *1-2 Chronicles, Ezra, Nehemiah*, volume 13 of *Old Testament Message* series.

---

Published in 1984 by: MICHAEL GLAZIER, INC., 1723 Delaware Avenue, Wilmington, Delaware 19806 and Dominican Publications, St. Saviour's, Dublin, Ireland.

©1984 by Céline Mangan, O.P. All rights reserved.

Library of Congress Catalog Card Number: 83-83255
International Standard Book Number:
    Ways of Prayer series: 0-89435-282-0
    CAN WE STILL CALL GOD "FATHER"?
        0-89435-384-3 (Michael Glazier, Inc.)
        0-907271-29-4 (Dominican Publications)

Cover art by Lillian Brulc
Typography by Richard Rein Smith
Printed in the United States of America

# CONTENTS

Introduction ............................... 7
1. Can We Still Call God "Father"? ........... 9
2. The Jewish Father....................... 18
3. Teach Us to Pray ....................... 29
4. What Does It Mean to "Hallow the Name"? ... 42
5. "God Rules OK"?........................ 54
6. The Good Pleasure of God ................ 67
7. God Gives Bread........................ 77
8. God Forgives .......................... 88
9. God and Evil .......................... 97
10. Into Your Hands....................... 106

# INTRODUCTION

A recent book on the Our Father heads its introductory chapter: "Not another Book on the Our Father." This was precisely my own reaction when I was asked to write on the Lord's Prayer for this series on *Ways of Prayer*. But it was pointed out to me that none of these books had been written by a woman, so I agreed to be persuaded.

Each person has his or her own commentary on the Our Father; I can only write out of my own background as an Irish Catholic religious woman who happens to be involved in scripture studies. Each of these components has contributed to my own story of prayer and to my discovery of the depths of the Our Father. Each of them is in a state of evolution (or even revolution) at the moment and I have to be continually aware of these changes if I am to remain true to the ongoing understanding of the prayer in today's world.

I have tried in the following pages to be sensitive to the exciting new insights women are bringing to the study of the scriptures. As the presuppositions of the past are being swept aside, new light is being shed on the role of women in the Bible and also on the understanding of the God portrayed there.

There is some negative, even violent, reaction to calling God, "Father" at all today and this will have to be examined.

My own approach to the Our Father will be largely scriptural; the Our Father, after all, is the whole of the Bible in miniature. I would like in particular to be aware of the Jewish background to the prayer. As this is a book on prayer rather than exegesis, however, I can take the many fine studies on the Our Father for granted while being aware of their findings and noting them where necessary.

What I have written, then, owes a lot to the scripture scholars, both men and women, who have worked in the field before me but it owes more, perhaps, to the many people with whom I have been involved in the various scripture groups with which I have been associated in the past few years. These have brought God's Word for me out of the books and into real life. I would like to thank them and to thank in particular Sister Denis O'Neill and Sister Pius Donnelly for their help with typing and proofreading. Finally, I owe a particular word of gratitude to Father Bill Riley for reading the manuscript and offering some valuable suggestions for improvement.

# 1

# Can We Still Call God "Father"?

> The Bible is no longer the book that stabilizes government and confirms the existing order. It has fallen into the hands of the powerless, and the question is what it has to say to them and what 'power' it gives them: a new old 'mastery,' or the power of those who remained by the cross.
>
> Elisabeth Moltmann-Wendel

The Our Father is the prayer most often used by us as Christians; from the day we learnt it, if not at our mother's knee at least in the first grade at school, until the day it is said over our coffins, it forms the hub of our prayer life. But for how many of us is it really a prayer? If it is to be so in a realistic way it must form part of our meaning as Christians today and an understanding of it must take into account the reality of contemporary concerns. This has always happened in the interpretation of the prayer. Looking at the commentaries on it down the centuries, it is interesting to see how each generation has refracted the essence of the prayer through the crystal of its own insights (and limitations).

St. Teresa of Avila's commentary, for instance, comes clothed in the thought patterns of the sixteenth century; Simone Weil's in those of the twentieth — and a twentieth century at war at that. Charles de Foucauld comments on it in the language of French spirituality of the turn of the century; his disciple, Carlo Carretto, in the more stark terms of the seventies. It seems to give special light in our age of uncertainty to those searching for a meaning to life: phrases from it constantly pointed the way ahead for Dag Hammarskjöld, while Michael Crosby, in the book whose opening chapter I mentioned in the Introduction, shows how the Our Father can challenge us to be involved in the social needs of our time.[1]

At the same time it has to be admitted that there is something of a malaise about the Our Father in many quarters today. What has a God who is seemingly solely male to offer to militant feminists? Or can the term, father, for God have any credibility anymore in the light of Freud's claim that we are all caught in the coils of an Oedipus complex? Must we hurl the Our Father back in God's face as many do who cannot experience the reality of the divine in their lives:

> Our Father who art in heaven stay there
> And we will stay on earth
> Which is at times so lovely
> With its mysteries of New York
> With its mysteries of Paris
> Which absolutely outweigh the mystery of the Trinity.[2]

---

[1] See M. Crosby, *Thy Will Be Done. Praying the Our Father as Subversive Activity*, Maryknoll, New York: Orbis Books, 1977.

[2] Quoted in J. J. Petuchowski and M. Brocke (eds.) *The Lord's Prayer and Jewish Liturgy*, London: Burns Oates, 1974, p. 184.

## "If God is male, then male is God"

This caustic comment on the theological situation today comes from Mary Daly, a thought provoking protagonist of the feminist movement, in a book significantly entitled, *Beyond God the Father*. It sums up the frustrations of many women today, faced as they are with male dominated churches.

> My difficulties about God as father, begetter, ruler and the manager of history grew as I began to understand more clearly what it means to be born a woman and therefore 'incomplete,' and so to have to live in a patriarchal society. How could I want power to be the dominant characteristic of my life? And how could I worship a God who was only a male?[3]

So writes Dorothee Sölle, a German theologian, whose distrust of the extremes of power associated with God stems from her experiences in the concentration camp of Auschwitz during World War II. She goes on:

> Male power, for me, is something to do with roaring, shooting and giving orders. I do not think that this patriarchal culture has done me any more damage than other women. It only became constantly more obvious to me that any identification with the aggressor, the ruler, the violator, is the worst thing that can happen to a woman.[3]

My own background would not give me such extreme reactions. Though it is true that the Irish Church is probably more chauvinistic than most, at a professional level I have

---

[3] D. Sölle, "Paternalistic Religion as Experienced by Women," *Concilium* 143(1981) 72.

always found myself accepted as an equal person within it. At the same time I feel the need to be 'conscientised' to the domination of the patriarchal model of the Church and the onesided identification of the father image for God with male dominated power structures. These are not only damaging to women but to men also, as they deprive the Church of at least half of its potential for understanding what is needed today. At a recent meeting in which a Catholic bishop was present, I happened to make a suggestion off the top of my head about the structures of parish life in the diocese. His rejoinder was that I was the third *woman* in the previous few weeks to make a similar suggestion.

> We must once again learn to think, feel, live and act in terms of a total sense of living. To do this, we shall have to rediscover a forgotten art to use our imagination in our theology. Theological imagination is necessary in a church and a theology which has lost touch with women, if new life is to be given to the gospel of liberation. With this kind of imagination, theology which has become abstract and has lost touch with women, can again become what it once was, and affect the whole person.[4]

The limiting of God as Father to male dominated power structures began very early in the Church's history. As we shall see, in the Bible many of the characteristics attributed to the father image for God are those which we assign to a mother. But by the time of the Apostle's Creed, God is being understood almost solely as, "Father Almighty, maker of

---

[4] E. Moltmann-Wendel, *The Women Around Jesus*, London: SCM, 1982, p. 9.

heaven and earth." This almighty image of God the Father smacks of the powerful patriarchal world view of the later Roman Empire to which Church leaders of the time were doing their level best to conform. It is so much with us still that a recent writer who wants to see how woman is in the image of God has to bypass God the Father and see herself in the image of the Spirit instead. Indeed many are beginning to use "she" for the Spirit. I do not go along with this, not only because in the Bible the Spirit is more associated with power than any of the other "persons" in the Godhead, but also because it gets the Father off the hook, as it were. We need to explore the father image itself and to realise how, especially in the Bible, it can be associated with concepts other than those of patriarchal power.

Even though there are some militant women today who would wish in their struggle for equality to put a female Mother Goddess in the place of an ousted Father God, the majority would not go that far as they would see this as merely substituting one domination for another. What they are seeking to explore is the reflection of the feminine in the Godhead itself and, as a consequence, an acknowledgement of the place of the feminine as part and parcel of our approach to God and therefore in Church structures.

We are becoming more and more aware, with the help of psychology, that all women have masculine traits and all men feminine. What is needed in all of us is a coming to terms with our opposite poles and an integration of them into our lives so that a greater potential for human growth and wholeness is released. It is increasingly being realised that Jesus was the only fully integrated person, the only one who had brought to maturity the masculine and feminine traits in his character. It was because of this that he could relate so easily to women and have no difficulty in seeing them as belonging to his followers. How he viewed God also was totally integrated and so an exploration of the scriptures, keeping in mind this integration, should help towards a deeper understanding of his use of the model of fatherhood for God and the wholeness that this model calls us to. This should be a means of deepening our image of God today and releasing the Father image of God for prayer again in our time.

## Models of fatherhood

> Perhaps contemporary theological discussion can move "Beyond God the Father" yet probably not in the sense that this model can be discarded but rather reinterpreted in a contemporary context.[5]

Father, of course, is not the only model for God. In the next chapter we will take a look at other models of God in the Bible, models which were far more frequently used than that of father. Today other models have more appeal, such as the divine "Thou" of Buber, the "ground of our being" of Tillich, the "beyond in our midst" of Bonhoeffer. It is not a question of either-or. Our experience of the Godhead is enriched if we keep many different understandings of it in tension with one another. But because the New Testament used "Father" so frequently as a designation of the God of Jesus, I doubt if we can have a Christianity that does not at least use the model of fatherhood as a major term of reference for God.

[5]W. Wifall, "Models of God in the Old Testament," *Biblical Theology Bulletin*, 9 (1979) 185.

But what do we mean when we use the term, father, for God today? It has to be admitted that we are heirs to models of fatherhood which do not go even as far back as the time of the early Church. The image of fatherhood has taken quite a battering in the past few centuries. Apart from the Freudian death conflict between father and son, there is the tradition of eighteenth century painting which portrayed God as a nice old man in the sky, more grandfather than father. The Victorian image of the "heavy" father has left us with more of a godfather image; one has only to think of the irrational authoritarianism portrayed by the father of the poetess, Elisabeth Barrett Browning, in the film version of her life: *The Barretts of Wimpole Street.*

The father image was that most commonly used in these centuries for any authority figure, lawgiver or ruler. It became linked with establishment images, with holding onto the status quo. It is no wonder, then, that with the breakdown of law and order and authority today, the Our Father is often thrown out the window, as a similar parody to the one already quoted suggests:

> Our Father who art neither in heaven nor on earth,
> Neither in the negro slums of Harlem
> Nor with the dead in Vietnam,
> Derided be thy name
> For thy blessing comes from nowhere,
> Thy curses roar at us
> And thou sendest us wars without warning.[6]

---

[6]Petuchowski, p. 183.

It has often been the experience of prison officers and others dealing with young people "in trouble," and trying to get some idea of God across to them, that the mere mention of God as father has been enough to turn them away from God forever, remembering as they do their own experiences of vindictive and drunken fathers. I know of one social educator who, when faced with an attitude like this in the young boys with whom she works, tries to help them to be a "father" to their own fathers. If this happens it can be a great source of healing and growth for the boys themselves and also for other members of their families. Of course this implies a totally different image of father than the authoritarian one, a caring image which brings out the best in a person. This has often been associated in the past with the mother in a family. But roles are changing and blurring in even the most traditional of families today. Especially where both parents are working, the parenting roles can be equally shared. As children grow, too, their parents tend to give them a share in family decision making, helping them to make choices so that they will gradually learn to exercise adult responsibility.

If the model of father used for God, therefore, continues to be largely paternalistic and authoritarian, there will be many today who will reject it, not only because it is downgrading of women but because this model breeds infantilism and the kind of submission which degrades rather than upbuilds. If, however, the more positive aspects of parenting, which include female as well as male attributes, are posited of God by the use of the word, "Father" then it is still an image which can speak to the people of our time.

## Summary

The divinity after all is neither male nor female but we have only human language in which to speak of God. It was probably inevitable, therefore, that male language dominated down the ages given the male dominated societies of the centuries. With the raising of consciousness among women the balance can be redressed and a whole new depth of our heritage rediscovered, not only for women but for men as well. This can only be of benefit to all of us in our search for the reality of God in prayer.

# 2
# The Jewish Father

It happened during the darkest time of the European tragedy, the effects of which are still felt. I was at that time an outlaw escaped abroad after many difficult experiences. I had surrendered and forgotten my identity. In 1944 I slid into an identity borrowed from a Franciscan monastery in Prescov... Then I discovered a token of this identity in the Lord's Prayer. That was like a Jewish prayer.

*B. Graubard*

It is only in very recent times that we Christians are discovering the Jewishness of Jesus and in that way laying ourselves open again to a whole area of our inheritance of which we had largely lost sight. Perhaps the greatest debt we owe to our Jewish past is the possibility of having a sense of God at all and consequently of being able to pray. As a Jewish rabbi puts it:

What a great wonder that man should be able to draw so near to God in prayer. How many walls there are between man and God! Even though God fills all the world, he is so very hidden! Yet a single word of prayer can topple all the walls.[1]

Jesus stood firmly in this great tradition of prayer and passed on to us his own insights and understanding of the God revealed through the Hebrew scriptures.

Why, however, did he pick "Father" as his special title for God? Why not one of the more common ways of looking at God which his people had made their own throughout their history? Why not, for example, *Savior, Creator* or *Lord*? By making use of an exclusively male title he has caused us some headaches in this century, as we have seen. Let us delay a little on some of these other Jewish ways of addressing God and see how they relate to Jesus' concept of God as Father.

## *Our Savior who art . . . ?*

Another great rediscovery of Christians at the present time is the realisation that salvation (or liberation) is at the heart of the biblical experience of God. It is an insight which our Jewish brothers and sisters have never lost. When the youngest member of a Jewish household asks at the feast of Passover every year: "Why is this night different from all other nights of the year?", the answer given is the saga of God's liberation of the people of Israel from Egypt. The Exodus for them was only the beginning of a journey into freedom, initially a freedom

---

[1] A. Green, B. W. Holtz (eds.) *Your Word is Fire*, New York: Paulist Press, 1977, p. 20.

*from* oppression and slavery but increasingly down through their history, a freedom *to* live their lives in keeping with the call of their faith.

Many a time throughout this history the people rebelled and tried to pin God down to their own limited ways of thinking and acting. Always when this happened God would break out of the mould in which they had placed him and a new liberation would occur. This pattern of *liberation — rebellion - new liberation* is reflected in the texts of the Bible which speak of God as savior and father in one breath:

*Liberation:*

You, Lord, are our father
our redeemer you are named forever (Is 63:16);

*Rebellion:*

Even now do you not call me, "My father,
you who are the bridegroom of my youth"?
"Will he keep his wrath forever,
Will he hold his grudge to the end?"
This is what you say, yet you do
all the evil you can (Jer 3:4-5);

*New Liberation:*

They departed in tears,
but I will console them and guide them;
I will lead them to brooks of water,
on a level road, so that none shall stumble,
for I am a father to Israel,
Ephraim is my first-born. (Jer 31:9)

As time went on the privileged relationship of father to son was seen to be that between God and the king who was looked on as the representative of the whole people. In the great inaugural speech which set up the Davidic monarchy, God speaks to the king through the prophet Nathan:

> I will be a Father to him
> and he shall be a son to me. (2 Sam 7:14)

But unlike the other nations of the time this did not mean for Israel that their king was a god, as the text quickly goes on to point out:

> And if he does wrong, I will correct him.

The king was just as much in need of being saved as everyone else. The psalmist makes him say:

You are my father, my God, the Rock, my savior. (Ps 89:26)

At the heart of the understanding of God in the Bible, then, is the realisation that the God of Israel is a God who wishes to save his people. The picture Jesus gives us of the Father with his arms wide open to receive back the prodigal son has its roots in this Old Testament image of God.

## Our Creator who art ... ?

Creator is probably the first idea that comes to the minds of Christians when they say *God*. This is not true of the people of the Bible. They were always conscious of God as savior even when speaking of him as creator. It was only late in their history that they came to the full realisation of God as their creator. This happened when their country was over-run and they were carted off as exiles to Babylon:

> All the symbols of Hebrew religion — city, temple, Ark, sacrifice, priesthood and land — died at once. God himself seemed to have died. 'Death of God' Theology is not a novelty.[2]

How often it happens that we have to let go of all the props surrounding God before we come to the knowledge of the true God.

The problem was that in ancient times it was believed that a God could only be worshipped in his own land. When the foreign army commander, Naaman, for example, was cured of leprosy by the prophet Elisha in Israel, he asked for two mule loads of Israelite earth to take home with him so that he could worship Israel's God upon it. So the people of Israel in exile could only lament:

> How could we sing a song of the Lord in a foreign land?
> (Ps 137:4)

Exile released God from bondage to the land and the people were eventually able to make the great leap of faith which led them to the full realisation that their God was also God of the whole world. They were not doomed to extinction; the future which was full of surprises, miracles and mystery belonged to their God as had the past.

There are a few passages in the Bible where the title, "Father" is linked to the idea of God as creator, but we have to

---

[2]B. Janecko, "Israel, Prophecy, Politics," *Biblical Theology Bulletin* 8 (1978) 178.

be careful to see these passages in the light of the link between God as creator and savior. In the Bible the mention of God as Father-Creator is in relation to his winning a people for himself rather than to making the world:

> Is he not your father who set you up?
> Has he not made you and established you (Deut 32:6).

He is reminded when they are in need of a new liberation that:

> Yet, O Lord, you are our father;
> We are the clay and you the potter:
> We are all the work of your hands. (Is 64:8)

They were in a covenant relationship with their Creator-Father and were not slow to remind him that he had obligations to look after them, even when they turned their backs on him. The other side of the coin held true too of course and one of the latest of the prophets, Malachi, reminded the people that fidelity to their Creator-Father was shown by their fidelity to one another:

> Have we not all one Father?
> Has not the one God created us?
> Why then do we break faith with each other,
> violating the covenant of our father? (Mal 2:10)

## Our Lord who art...?

After the return from Exile the people, conscious that it had been their own sinfulness which had brought about their downfall, developed a much more reverential attitude towards

God. Instead of continuing to call him *Yahweh*, their own special name for him since the time of Moses, they began to think and speak of him by the more deferential title, Lord.

> Praise him, you Israelites, before the Gentiles,
> for though he has scattered you among them,
> he has shown his greatness even there.
> Exalt him before every living being,
> because he is the Lord our God,
> our Father and God forever. (Tobit 13:3-4)

Even when they called him, Lord, however, they continued to stress the saving aspects of his relationship with them. The above passage shows that this is again linked with the idea of God as father. In the past, the saving was shown to the people as a whole. In the Wisdom Books, one of the latest sections of the Bible to be written, it could be applied to each individual person:

> I called out: O Lord, you are my father,
> you are my champion and my savior;
> do not abandon me in time of trouble,
> in the midst of storms and dangers. (Sir 51:10; see 23:1-8)

In such a passage, though the title, Lord, is used for God, it is clear that by the fact that it is coupled with "Father" and "Savior" the intimate relationship between God and his own is not broken. He is particularly Lord of those in need:

> Sing to God, chant praise to his name,
> extol him who rides upon the clouds,
> Whose name is the Lord,
> exult before him,

The father of orphans and the defender of widows
is God in his holy dwelling.    (Ps 68:4-6)

One aspect of this saving relationship is that of forgiveness. Psalm 103, for example, speaks of that forgiveness in terms of a father's love:

As far as the east is from the west,
so far has he put our transgressions from us,
as a father has compassion on his children,
so the Lord has compassion on those who fear him.    (Ps 103:12-13)

Just before the time of Jesus there was a great hope abroad among the Jewish people that God would come in a new way to renew his people. Part of that coming would be a great outpouring of forgiveness. The same Father who had been patient and forgiving when his people had turned away in the past would know how to be creative in a new age.

## Our Mother who art . . . ?

If the male image of God is the most predominant in the Bible, that is not to say that more feminine characteristics are not also present. The more obvious passages are often quoted, for example:

But Zion said, "The Lord has forsaken me;
my Lord has forgotten me."
Can a mother forget her infant,
be without tenderness for the child of her womb?
Even should she forget
I will never forget you.    (Is 49:14-15)

Many of the father passages we have been considering indeed show also the care and tenderness of a mother for a very young child:

> When Israel was a child I loved him,
> out of Egypt I called my son...
> Yet it was I who taught Ephraim to walk,
> who took them in my arms;
> I drew them with human cords,
> with bands of love;
> I fostered them like one
> who raises an infant to his cheeks;
> Yet though I stooped to feed my child,
> they did not know that I was their healer. (Hos 11:1-4)

In some of these passages both masculine and feminine words are used together to portray God's power in relation to the people; Deut 32, for example, which speaks of God as a "father who created you," goes on to portray the relationship between God and the people in the beautiful imagery of a mother bird teaching her young to fly:

> As an eagle incites its nestlings forth
> by hovering over its brood,
> so he spread his wings to receive them
> and bore them up on his pinions.

Luke has Jesus use this imagery in his distress over the people of Jerusalem's lack of sensitivity to the insight into God which he was presenting to them (see Lk 13:34-35).

It is interesting to note that the word, "helper," used of Eve in Genesis (2:18), is ascribed to God elsewhere in the Bible:

> Hear then, O Jacob, my servant,
> Israel, whom I have chosen.
> Thus says the Lord who made you,
> Your *helper*, who formed you from the womb:
> Fear not, O Jacob, my servant,
> the darling whom I have chosen. (Is 44:1-2)

Again the words used here are very much in the feminine mould: God is involved with the womb, with cherishing and making a darling of his people, in this case specifically chosen to be an instrument of God's mission to the world.

The image of God as parent is expanded in later Jewish writings. From before the time of Jesus we find, for example, in the Dead Sea Scrolls:

> As a woman who tenderly loves her babe
> do you rejoice in them;
> and as a foster father bearing a child in his lap
> so do you care for all your creatures.

From later Jewish liturgical writings we get an image of God in the activity which became the heart of Judaism: giving the Torah, the Law to his people, portrayed in a very womanly way:

> God drew out the Torah for me
> as a mother draws out her breast for her child.

It would be difficult to get better images than these of the closeness of God to his people and his care and concern that they be nourished and protected. The parenting images of God, though used sparingly enough in the Jewish tradition, were right at the heart of the people's understanding of their

God. These images are far nearer to present day democratic images of the supporting roles of parents in families than they are to the authoritarian images of centuries gone past. Jesus, by greatly expanding the use of Father in particular for God, but also being open to motherly characteristics, threw wide open for us the way which led again into the heart of God.

## Summary

The title, "Father," for God as used in the Hebrew scriptures and in later Jewish writings, brought out the depth of his tender care and compassion for the people in a power to save, renew and forgive. In these texts, characteristics which are considered exclusively feminine are attributed to God indiscriminately. The fact that father is used of God only about fifteen times in the Hebrew scriptures implied a certain hesitancy about applying it. Jesus would have no such hesitancy; "Father" became his favourite way of addressing God.

# 3

# Teach Us to Pray

When the world needed rain, our teachers used to send schoolchildren to the holy man who seized the hem of his coat and said to him: "Abba, abba, give us rain." He said to God: "Master of the Universe grant the rain for the sake of those who are not yet able to distinguish between an *abba* who has the power to give rain and an *abba* who has not.

*Jewish Talmud*

*Abba*, as is well known, was the word for father in the language Jesus spoke. More correctly it should be translated as, "my dear Father" or "Daddy." Jesus used the close relationship between father and child as his preferred way of showing us what God is like and how we are to approach him. We are to go to God with unaffected simplicity as a child runs to its Daddy.

By calling God, *Abba*, then Jesus took up the connotations of tenderness which, as we have seen, were already present in the Hebrew scriptures. The word probably originated from the babblings of baby talk. It was not used before the time of

Jesus for God. The holy man quoted at the beginning of this chapter is careful to call God, "Master of the Universe," when he himself is addressing him, though he allows that children who might not know better could perhaps think of God as *Abba*. Any self-respecting rabbi, however, would call him, "Master of the Universe."

This gives us a clue to at least part of the meaning of Jesus' own statement that we must become as little children to enter the kingdom of God. In our relationship to God we must have the total simplicity and trust of a small child toward its parents. The psalmist talks of being "like a weaned child on its mother's lap" (Ps 131:2). The point about this is that it is a *weaned* child which is in question, not a tiny infant. The image the psalmist presents is of a two or three year old who has been toddling around, up to all kinds of mischief. It suddenly gets tired and dashes itself into its mother's arms, peevish and fretful. The mother rubs it down and smooths it into a quiet peacefulness and contentment. We come to the Lord out of all kinds of mischief maybe, and full of restlessness and anxiety. Instead of feeling guilty, we must learn to allow ourselves to be soothed and quietened so that we can hear what God has to say to us.

## Pushed into living

*Abba*, however, was not only a word used by young children in Jesus' time. Just as a grown person today will still say "Dad," so too *Abba* was used for the relationship between growing-up son or daughter as well as for that between pupil and teacher. It connotated then the father as the source of life, but also as the pattern of how to live out that life. By calling God, *Abba*, Jesus presents him to us as the one who spurs us beyond ourselves, who pulls forth the potential for life as every parent / teacher should do for a young person. As well as the tender, loving care aspect of parental love, therefore, there is also this pushing forth into life, this being drawn beyond oneself, which can be a very painful process indeed.

There is a beautiful picture of this process in Herman Hesse's book, *The Glass Bead Game*. The Rainmaker in an African village trains his disciple in his art:

> Something drew him to the old man, though he himself did not know what it was. Sometimes the Rainmaker would pretend not to notice. Sometimes he growled ungraciously and ordered the boy to make himself scarce. But sometimes he would beckon him and let him stay for the day, would assign him tasks, show him one thing and another, give him advice, tell him the name of plants, order him to draw water or kindle fire... Turu had submitted; he had allowed Knect to conquer him by tenacious courtship. Now he wished nothing more than to make a good rainmaker of the boy.

The gospels give us fascinating glimpses into Jesus' own "tenacious courtship" of God as he learnt to be "about his Father's business," learnt through temptation and struggle what doing the will of the Father meant. In his own prayer he had to seek for the true face of his Father for the time in which he lived. This would lead him to see which parts of his people's heritage were ripe for a new understanding of God and which had become dead wood.

God, like a good parent / teacher, taught him the secrets of his craft so that Jesus was enabled to pass on those secrets and to craft others in his work. What was that work? It was to reveal the true heart of God afresh to the people of his time and to call them to respond. By his own response Jesus showed his identity as son. By calling God, *Abba*, he was making an implicit assertion about who he himself was and about his own peculiar relationship to God.

## "Power: cherishing and making free"

This is how one modern theologian describes the kind of God Jesus was revealing to the people of his time. It would seem like a contradiction in terms as the last thing we think of power doing is cherishing and experience shows that very seldom is it that it makes free. But power in itself, apart from its abuse, can be a very positive thing. In itself it is energy, capacity for producing an effect or the moving force of anything. The dynamic energy and force which we are to see active behind our world is not the titanic forces which war and hatred unleash but an ability to "cherish and make free." Out of his experience of God as *Abba*, Jesus shows that true power consists of the gentle persuasive force of liberation through cherishing. He himself took that same road even when it inevitably led to his death.

It would seem to me that this way of presenting God's power as cherishing and making free has been most cultivated down the centuries by the feminine side of the human race and would certainly have been a better basis for relating to the world than the power structures of domination which the Church took over very early in its history, as we have seen. Jesus revealed a God who cherished the sick, the poor, the prostitutes and urged to freedom from sin and possessions those who, like the tax collectors, were weighed down by both. He did not see the necessity of setting up any vast programs, power structures or political parties to carry out the work of his Father. Instead, by his teaching, his deeds and his prayers, he exposed what God is like and invited his followers to learn the craft of God as he did. He handed over his most prized possession: his own name for God, *Abba*, to the rather disreputable band of followers who gathered about him and taught them to use it as their very own approach to God.

## *Teach us to pray*

What did those early followers of Jesus do with the precious heritage he left them? A look at their writings will give us some clues as to how they carried out his wish that they, too, could call God, *Abba*. They were conscious that this gave them a new relationship to God:

> All who are led by the Spirit of God are sons of God.
> You did not receive a spirit of slavery leading you back into fear,
> But a spirit of adoption through which we cry out: "Abba"
> (Rom 8:14-15).

This new relationship gave them the right to have a very affectionate approach to God, to have total confidence in the *Abba* of Jesus.

Religious groups of all times tend to have their own special prayers. The Our Father very soon became the special prayer of Jesus' early followers. It was reserved for those who were full members of the Church and was first said at the Communion after Baptism. The *Teaching of the Twelve Apostles*, one of the earliest Christian writings apart from the New Testament, speaks of the Our Father being said "three times a day." The Jews were accustomed to say prayers three times a day and so the Our Father was very early on substituted for these Jewish prayers as the Christians' very own prayer. The Jewish prayers said in Jesus' time were very beautiful. They consisted of the recitation of the *Shema*, the words of Deut 6, which is a great call to love and obey God:

> Hear, O Israel! The Lord is our God, the Lord alone!
> Therefore, you shall love the Lord, your God, with all your heart, and with all your soul and with all your strength...

Surrounding this were several long thanksgiving prayers which thanked God for the wonders he had done for his people in the past and begged his blessing in the present. Praise was also an essential ingredient of the prayers. The early Christians appreciated these lovely prayers but they soon realised that the Our Father contained them all within a very short compass. Maybe we fail to give it the centrality in our lives which they saw it as having by right.

Today, in the new Rite for the Christian Initiation of Adults, the Our Father is presented to the catechumens in a solemn ceremony, thus highlighting the fact that it is the special prayer of Christians. The wonder of having this special prayer is vividly brought out in the words of the Mass: "We have the courage to say" which is said before the solemn recitation of the Lord's Prayer by all present. We do not take it casually on ourselves to pray to God so intimately. It is a great gift that has been given to us. Perhaps the prayer is so familiar that we do not delay often enough on the giftedness of it. Through it we are given the power to enter into the concerns which animated Jesus' own prayer and to make those concerns our own; saying the Our Father daily, therefore, is a catechesis on what praying is all about.

## The Our Father in the gospels

It was in the Liturgy, then, that the Our Father was handed on and we find this reflected in the way it is presented in the gospels. It is only to be found in Matthew and Luke and in both it forms part of a catechesis on prayer. Since Matthew was writing primarily for Jews who had become Christians he could take it for granted that they were praying already but not perhaps in the right way:

> When you are praying, do not behave like the hypocrites who love to stand and pray in the synagogues or on street corners in order to be noticed... Whenever you pray, go to your room, close your door and pray to your Father in private. Then your Father, who sees what no man sees, will repay you. In your prayer do not rattle on like the pagans. They think they will win a hearing by the sheer multiplication of words. Do not imitate them. Your Father knows what you need before you ask him. This is how you are to pray: Our Father in heaven...
> (Mt 6:5-13)

In other words, prayer is not to be used as a means of bargaining with God or of bringing ourselves on an ego trip. The Our Father too is not to be confined to solemn worship but is to form the basis of our private prayer.

This injunction comes across even more strongly in Luke's version of the prayer. The wording in Luke is different from that of Matthew. This should come as no surprise to us since the early Christians were not as concerned about accurate transmission of mere words as we would be in a tape recorder and computer age. They were so conscious of having the Spirit of Jesus with them that they saw him as addressing their own needs and in Luke's largely Gentile church the needs were very different from Matthew's Jewish one. Matthew could take prayer for granted; Luke's church had to be encouraged to pray and to call God, *Abba*, and so the teaching on prayer in which the Our Father is enshrined in Luke is an admonition to be very free with God in prayer. Following on the giving of the Our Father to the disciples there is that beautiful story about the man banging on the door of his friend's house at night to get bread for a guest (Luke 11:5-13). The original point of the story is brought out in the following translation:

> Can you imagine if one of you had a friend and he had come to you at midnight and said to you: "Friend give me three loaves for a friend of mine on a journey has come to me and I have nothing to set before him" — that you would answer: "Go away and leave me in peace" — Can you imagine that? Of course not.

Not in the book of eastern hospitality that is and so Luke is saying that the kind of God *Abba* is, is a helpful and dependable friend who leans towards his people. On their side they have to keep faith and confidence in him and this is the point Luke is making about the continual banging on the door. Insistent prayer achieves its object in spite of difficulties; faith is kept alive by such prayer and the reward is the gift of the Spirit.

Many scholars would say that the Our Father in Luke's gospel is not only linked to this parable which comes after it but also to the preceeding story of Martha and Mary (10:38-42). Too often in the past Martha and Mary have been contrasted as the ideals of the active and the contemplative lives. But in the story, Martha is not held up as a model of discipleship at all so there can be no contrasting of two ways of following the Lord here. Elsewhere Martha is the dynamic example of faith in the Resurrection (see Jn 11:17-27) but not here.

Historically Mary of Bethany was probably the one disciple who understood something of what was happening in Jesus and who acted as a sounding board for him in the deepening understanding of his mission. Luke praises Mary's sensitivity to Jesus' concerns and holds her up as a model of what the disciple should be about. The "one thing" which she has chosen is precisely the content of the Our Father: concern for the Father's kingdom and his will which are the deepest concerns of Jesus.

## Father and Son

The more they thought about what had happened in Jesus the more excited the early Christians became, especially when they realised that the same God who had been active in their Jewish past with "mighty deeds and outstretched hand" was now present in the life of a seemingly ordinary man. From there they went on to realise that this man was God's Son in a special way and therefore shared in all the prerogatives of God:

> In times past, God spoke in fragmentary and varied ways through the prophets; in this, the final age, he has spoken to us through his Son, whom he made heir of all things and through whom he first created the universe. This Son is the reflection of the Father's glory, the exact representation of the Father's being, and he sustains all things by his powerful word. (Heb 1:1-3)

John's gospel does not have the Our Father but it is the one which contains most references to the relationship between the Father and the Son. The Son is the Word of God for John. In the Old Testament, the Word stood for the dynamic activity of God; when God spoke something happened. Now with the coming of Jesus that activity of God is present in a human person. We are to see in the words and works of Jesus the kind of God with whom we are to relate.

For John the real problem of human beings is not so much sin as ignorance — ignorance of who God really is. This is why he portrays Jesus as continually being misunderstood. Perhaps the greatest problem about the way we practise religion is our almost perennial capacity to obscure the real God and to shield ourselves from the truth of what facing reality involves. John in his gospel tries to draw back the veil of the revelation of God in the life of Jesus so that we will truly understand the heart of God as Father:

> No one has ever seen God;
> It is the only Son, who is nearest to the Father's heart,
> Who has made him known.
>     (Jn 1:18 — Jerusalem Bible Translation)

## Suffering and the Father

In Mark's gospel God appears as *Abba* only where Jesus gives himself over to suffering. This is especially true of Mark's account of the Agony in the Garden which has so many similarities with the Our Father. The Son took on himself the rebellion of human beings against the vision of universal peace which belief in a father God should bring with it. As an old Irish saying puts it:

> That dear youth had his breast pierced,
> for children whose love for their Father had grown cold.[1]

When one tries to become a peacemaker between two warring factions and has a hand on the shoulder of each, one can be torn asunder on the cross between the two.

But the question has often been asked: Where was the Father when Jesus was on the cross and, following on from that, where is he when we, too, are suffering? I think many of us still have an image of the Father at the Passion as a vindictive God making his Son conform to his brutal will. Or else we see the Passion itself as a necessary act to make up to God's flouted justice. Rather than considering God as someone to be placated, however, some recent writers would go so far as to stress the involvement of the whole Trinity in the Passion. "Whoever has seen me has seen the Father" (Jn 14:9) must be as true on Calvary as it was for the remainder of the life of Jesus. The designation of God as Father must surely

---

[1] Quoted in D. O'Laoghaire, "Being Part of God's Family: An aspect of Irish Spirituality," *Doctrine and Life*, 1983, 30.

suggest the agony of a bereaved parent rather than the vindictiveness of an aggrieved master. Many of us who have seen the heart-rending scenes at the graveside of victims of violence in recent years would find the image of God as a bereaved parent a very telling one indeed. Ian Paisley, one of the more prominent spokespersons for sectarianism in Northern Ireland, could yet go so far as to say at one such funeral:

> The tears of a Roman Catholic mother are just as precious in the eyes of God the Almighty as the tears of a Protestant mother.

I think that, in relation to the Passion, the best image we can come up with for God is to speak of the helplessness of the Father, the helplessness of a rejected parent whose love has been spurned. Too often our image of God is of a slot machine; we pray to be delivered from this suffering and that, and get angry when God does not hear our prayers. Should we not rather see God as the one who is with us in our sufferings, anguishing over us through the darkness. There is a passage in the writings of the Jewish rabbis which speaks of God going down to Exile in chains with his people. The text adds: "If one dare say such a thing." But I think we must dare, because it is only if we do that we come close to the God whom Jesus revealed to his followers as *Abba*. It is only if we consent to allow him to be with us in the suffering that we will come through with him to the wonder of new life and Resurrection.

> Is it possible to say what particular aspect of the incarnation is holding men's hearts today and shaping their lives? ... I would venture that it is precisely that of Christ crucified in weakness, the wisdom and the power of God; the revelation of God in the face of Christ Jesus delivered up to weakness and to

death. This is the mystery of God who is no benevolent almighty lavishing gifts on his creatures from afar, but love seeking intimacy, love that does not shout in the market place but whispers in the heart; love that is vulnerable, delivered into our hands to dispose of as we choose.[2]

## Summary

Jesus is shown in the New Testament to bypass the more usual Old Testament titles for God, such as *Savior, Creator, Lord*; instead the title "Father" comes to the fore, in particular the very familiar word for Father, *Abba*. Interestingly enough, Jesus' followers very soon began to apply the other titles for God to Jesus himself. He is seen as a savior and is several times called "Lord" and is spoken of as involved in creation. Jesus takes over the dynamic action of God on behalf of his people which had been shown forth in the past by great feats of creation and liberation. This same power is now shown however in the weakness of a man hanging on a cross with a seemingly helpless Father looking on:

> For God's folly is wiser than men,
> and his weakness more powerful than men.
> (1 Cor 1:25)

Our consideration of the petitions of the Our Father will tease out how we are to respond in prayer and in life to such a God.

---

[2]Ruth Burrows, *Guidelines for Mystical Prayer*, London: Sheed and Ward, 1976, p. 4.

# 4

# What Does It Mean to "Hallow the Name"?

> We are made of desire; but the desire which nails us down to what is imaginary, temporal, selfish can, if we make it pass wholly into this petition, become a lever which will tear us from the imaginary into the real and from time into eternity and will lift us right out of the prison of self.
>
> Simone Weil, *Waiting on God*

In the ancient world the name stood for the whole person; to know someone's name meant to have a certain control over that person. There are stories of kings, for instance, writing the names of their enemies on broken bits of pottery and then jumping up and down on them until they were broken in pieces. By this symbolioc gesture they hoped to gain victory over the said enemies. One did not lightly hand over one's name, then, in the ancient world. In the story of Jacob's wrestling with the angel, for example, the one with whom he wrestled will not reveal his name (Gen 32:23-33). One meaning of the Israelite special name for God, *Yahweh*, which can be translated as, "I am who I am," was: "I am keeping my name to myself, thank you." But there are other more profitable — for us — meanings to that name, as we shall see.

A name was not something to be bandied about, therefore, and in the Bible we find much talk about not profaning the name of God and keeping it holy. This probably conjures up for us a picture of someone going to Confession and saying: "I took the name of the Lord in vain ten times." Idly swearing on God's name for the sake of emphasis is not something to be recommended but neither is it the whole of what is to be condemned in the passages of the Bible which speak about profaning the name of God. Leviticus 18:21, for example, says:

> You shall not offer any of your offspring
> to be immolated to Molech,
> thus profaning the name of your God.

Child sacrifice was common practice with the people among whom the Israelites settled. But passages like this show that they were not to follow the example of these people. It would be an insult to the name of their God to think that he would demand such a thing.

Child sacrifice was wiped out of their customs fairly early in the people of Israel's history but there were many other ways by which they could be seen to profane God's name. Ezekiel 36:23, for instance, speaks of Israel profaning God's name among the Gentiles. How did they profane the name? The context shows it was by their evil deeds:

> When the house of Israel lived in their land,
> they defiled it by their conduct and deeds. (v. 17)

The content of these evil deeds is amply catalogued elsewhere in the prophets, for example in Amos:

> They trample the heads of the weak
> into the dust of the earth,
> and force the lowly out of the way.
> Son and father go to the same prostitute,
> profaning my holy name.   (Amos 2:7)

Profaning the name of God can have a lot more to do with actions against one's fellow human beings in the Bible than those directly against God himself. In effect it means that evil actions towards others obscure the face of the real God and so profane his name. Conversely, we honour God when we do good towards all his creatures.

## *A jealous God*

When the name "Jealous God" is used in the Bible it is in this sense that it has to be seen. He is a God who is concerned about his image, as it were. How is he represented? What kind of a God is he shown to be? The way the people live out their lives as his children shows what kind of God they are dealing with. It is in the context of the ten commandments, therefore, that he is often spoken of as a jealous God (see Ex 20:5). Rather than laws to be obeyed these are much more to be seen as concerned with the right relationship between God and the people and the people among themselves. "Keeping holy the Sabbath day" is not just about having a pious day for God but ensuring that one's employees have space to live a human life:

> Take care to keep holy the Sabbath day as the Lord, your God, commanded you. Six days you may labor and do all your work; but the seventh day is the Sabbath of the Lord, your God. No work may be done then, whether by you, or your son or daughter, or your male or female slave, or your ox or your ass or any of your beasts, or the alien who lives with you...
> (Deut 5:12-14)

We must not make a God of productivity. This can be seen also in the fourth commandment, "Honour your Father and your Mother" which, it should be remembered, is a commandment addressed like all the others to adults rather than to children. Even when people are no longer of use in a society they are not to be discarded. The remainder of the commandments likewise points up the need to show reverence to others if we are to honour God.

But the temptation for the people of Israel, as for all of us, was to pay lip service to God's name while going their own way in the ordinary events of life. At several different stages of their history they confined their service of God to external worship. God alway broke out of such a straitjacket, often in a blazing fire of anger from the mouth of one of the prophets. This is what lies behind the speech of Jeremiah at the gate of the Temple in Jerusalem as the people assembled piously to worship, feeling secure in the knowledge that as long as they had the Temple in their midst they were safe from the enemies who were nearly at their gates:

> Here you are, putting your trust in deceitful words to your own loss! Are you to steal and murder, commit adultery and perjury, burn incense to Baal, go after strange gods you know not, and yet come to stand before me in this house which bears

my name and say: "We are safe; we can commit all these abominations again"? Has this house which bears my name become in your eyes a den of thieves? I too see what is being done, says the Lord. (Jer 7:8-11)

God's jealousy then is not so much for himself as that his people will understand what relationship to him is all about. Response to God of its very nature involves responsibility for one another. Charles de Foucauld sums it up beautifully in his commentary on the Our Father when he says:

> For the revealing of your glory
> and the making perfect of men
> is one and the same thing.[1]

## *I am with you*

The God at the root of biblical experience is, therefore, one who is totally turned towards his people. This is borne out in the other meanings of the special name, *Yahweh*, with which they named him. This is a word whose true meaning was largely lost sight of for centuries in the Christian Church. In the light of western philosophical thinking, it was translated as "I am" meaning, "I exist," "I am the only totally necessary being." But the people of the Bible could not have thought in this abstract way and so what the name, *Yahweh*, implied for them was that God was there for his people: "I am the one you will see me to be — when I lead you out of Egypt, into the

---

[1] C. de Foucauld, *Come Let Us Sing a Song Unknown*, Denville: Dimension, p. 18.

desert, into the promised land — I will be with you always."
All that God was to mean for his people was summed up in
this name.

It was Moses who drew from God this revelation of God's
name for his people. The story from the early chapters of
Exodus is very familiar; it is a story which begins with the cry
of a people in distress:

> As their cry for release went up to God,
> he heard their groaning and was mindful of his covenant.
>
> (Ex 2:24)

It is amazing the number of times in the Bible that God is
shown to answer immediately his people's cry for help. It is as
if God's hands are tied until the people take the initiative and
then the response is immediate. Maybe the Bible gives here a
profound psychological insight:

> Human cries ... convey meanings that have more depth than
> their immediate apparent contents ... A baby cries "for his
> feed," but in the eyes of an adult observer his need extends to
> the full tenderness of his mother's love, a love that is essential
> to his development, and one that he will continue to claim long
> after having learned to find his milk independently. Thus the
> prayer-cry symbolises something other than itself ... it is
> expressive of human desires experienced in the relation with
> God and seeking to harmonise with his plan for the world.[2]

In the Book of Exodus it is the basic cry for deliverance
from slavery which is in question. Moses had earlier seen the
difficulties his people were in and had tried off his own bat to do

---

[2] A. Godin (ed.) *From Cry to Word*, Brussels: Lumen Vitae, 1968, p. 21.

something about them but he had failed (Ex 2:11-15). He needed a time of deepening and testing before becoming the person who would mediate the revelation of God's name to his people. Alone in the desert he had time to reflect, becoming as D. H. Laurence so beautifully puts it in his poem, *Thought*: "A man in his wholeness wholly attending." This attentiveness and his ability to "turn aside" (Ex 3:3) made him receptive to God's call to become the liberator of his people. But now the one who was so eager to rush in and save them becomes hesitant and unsure of himself. It needs all God's assistance to make him take up the task in his name.

Ever afterwards throughout their history the people of Israel felt defended by the name of God. This comes across very much in the Psalms where, in prayer, they remind God that the name he has means that he is obliged to defend them:

> Help us, O God our savior,
> because of the glory of your name;
> Deliver us and pardon our sins,
> for your name's sake.    (Ps 79:9)

Forgiveness of sins is linked with the name in this passage. Conscious of their ability to profane the name of God by their sinfulness they ask for forgiveness from the God who has handed over his name to them.

## Blessing the name

Seeing what God has done and will do for his people results in their "blessing" him and his name. Blessing God, when we stop to think of it, seems a contradiction in terms. Surely it is

God who should bless us. But because of what he has done for them in the past the people saw God's name as "blessable," that is, worthy of praise and thanksgiving. This blessing God is often a spontaneous outburst of joy at who God is and thanksgiving for his ways with his people. You can see many examples of this in the Psalms and in other Jewish writings from before the time of Jesus, for example in the Ded Sea Scrolls, *Hymns of Thanksgiving*, we find:

> I will sing of your mercies
> and on your might I will meditate all day long.
> I will bless your name for ever
> and my soul shall delight in your great goodness.

Reverencing the name of God, then, means thanking him for his goodness, being part of that goodness oneself, and proclaiming it to others. Jesus used this blessing type of prayer when one day in a great outburst of joy he thanked the Father for revealing himself to the little people of his time (see Mt 11:25-30). They alone understood what it meant to reverence God's name in true fashion.

In later Jewish writings the whole of the Bible was seen as nothing but the revelation of the great and holy name of God. The main purpose in life, of those in the Jewish mystical tradition in particular, was to unlock the mystery of that name and so to enter into union with God. Great systems of prayer were drawn up for doing this. One of them was to take the ten most common attributes of God in the Old Testament, for example, his knowledge, his mercy, his kindness, and to use them as symbolic words, repeated in such a way as to bring one into the presence of God. In a sense this is not unlike the use of a mantra, familiar to us today from Eastern meditation, in which the use of a word repeated over and over again brings one into an atmosphere of prayer.

In passing it can be noted that many of the attributes of God thus mentioned were considered as feminine, his presence for example, as the following prayer testifies:

> As a person begins his prayer, reciting the words
>   "O Lord, open my lips,
>   and let my mouth declare your praise"
>   the Presence of God comes into him.
> Then it is the presence herself
>   who commands his voice;
> One who knows in faith
>   that all this happens within him
>   will be overcome with trembling
>   and with awe.[3]

## Jesus and the democratisation of God's name

In Jesus' own time the name of God, *Yahweh*, had become too sacred to pronounce and so words like *Lord, Holy One*, or even *Name* itself were used as a substitute for it. God in a way had become remote again. The very name which was meant to reveal him as being with us could no longer be pronounced. Matthew's gospel preserves something of this Jewish caution when it qualifies "Father" by "Who art in heaven." By doing so, however, it gives us one of the best statements about God ever formulated. We have a God who is "Our Father," very close and very dear to us, but also one who is "in heaven,"

[3] *Your Word is Fire*, p. 61.

transcendent. The human tendency is to exaggerate one or other of these aspects: to make him too remote as the Jews of Jesus' time tended to do; or to turn God into a cosy manageable entity, a trap our times can readily fall into. The truth is in the tension between intimacy and transcendence and Christianity is at its best when it holds onto the reality of that tension.

Jesus in his own time needed to release the name of God from the remoteness to which it had been relegated. He revealed again a God who is *Emmanuel*, "God with us" (Mt 1:23). He was not denying his Jewish heritage when he gave the new name, *Abba*, to God. The whole Old Testament realisation of God's concern to save his people which was contained in the name, *Yahweh*, was subsumed under the name, *Abba*, and made accessible in a new way. Hallowing the name did not mean for Jesus, keeping it locked up, sacred, untouchable, never to be pronounced. We must surely take seriously Jesus' stance towards the untouchables of his society: the lepers, sinners, prostitutes, tax collectors. It was to them that he entrusted the name, *Abba*, as we have seen, and allowed it to be used by them, presumably running the risk of having it bandied about in the not too polite society in which he mixed. It was from out of this society that *Abba* found its way into the early church.

Jesus prayed for his own that they would be protected by God's name and said that he himself had guarded them with his Father's name (Jn 17: 11-12). They were the ones who would have his name written on their foreheads (Rev 14:1). They, in their turn, would receive a new name (Rev 2:17) which would be a sign of their rebirth in Christ. This is what lies behind the giving of a new name to a catechumen at

Baptism. The newly baptised in their turn are to act like Jesus in revealing the name of God to others so that they, too, can live by it and hallow it.

To "hallow" God's name, then, is to have respect for him but also to have respect for all his people. One of the great losses in our industrialised world is that of a person's name. People become numbers on a card to be clocked in and clocked out; entered on tax forms and redundancy slips. There is great need again to cherish people by their names and this is what many movements within the Churches are trying to do. One of the first things that struck me about the charismatic movement, for instance, was the way everyone was on first name terms and you were cherished just because you were who you were and nobody else. This is one of the great gifts, too, of the followers of Charles de Foucauld; to live an ordinary life in a neighbourhood and to know the people around and in the factory by their names. To address someone by his or her own name gives that person identity and sacredness again.

## Summary

In this petition of the Our Father we are asking that we might know truly who the Father is — in the full biblical sense of *to know* which has connotations of experience more than of knowledge. Jesus, by allowing us to take his name for God on our lips, opens up the fullness of his insight into God to us. We hallow the name when we enter into that fullness and in turn bring others to it. We profane the name when we obscure the true nature of God; when our actions stem from selfishness and evil. Hallowing the name of God also involves having a respect for the name and person of each of our brothers and sisters.

# 5
# "God Rules OK"?

> One of the marks of a true dialectician is the ability to "move beyond" the past, without repudiating it in the name of new levels of critical consciousness presently enjoyed.
>
> *Paolo Freire*

In my own experience of helping people to understand and pray the scriptures, I have found that one of the greatest stumbling blocks they have is with the concept of the kingdom of God. Our age is largely out of sympathy with monarchy or even authority of any kind. Indeed the graffiti world has turned the word *rule* upside down; the power is no longer to come from the top down but is vested in the local leader who has the ability to bring people with him.

Without pressing the analogy too far there is something of this in what Jesus did with the concept of kingdom in his day. He burst wide open the way in which it was understood in the received tradition, yet at the same time, in the words of Paolo Freire, he did not repudiate that tradition. Rather, he took the essence of the idea of the kingdom and released it for the people of his own time.

In the language of the Bible what is behind the notion of God's kingdom is the recognition that God *is* God, that ultimately he is the one source of life and reality. Many of the prayers of the Jewish liturgy had a strong sense of this reality, for example the great *Kaddish* prayer which proclaims the glory of God and has many echoes in the Our Father:

> Exalted and hallowed be his great Name in the world which he created according to his will. May he establish his Kingdom in your lifetime and in your days, and in the lifetime of the whole household of Israel speedily and at a near time.[1]

Jesus' contemporaries would have agreed with his emphasis on God's kingdom but the various parties within Judaism at the time had different interpretations as to how it should be realised in practice. The *Sadducees*, for example, the largely priestly group which controlled the (lucrative) Temple worship, were happy enough with the status quo of Roman rule. As long as tithes were being paid and the ceremonial liturgy of the Temple carried out, they saw no reason to doubt that God was sovereign of his land even if the Romans had political control over it. The *Essenes*, largely in anger at the avarice with which Temple worship was being conducted (see Jn 2:13-22), rejected it and set themselves apart by a life of prayer, asceticism and study to await the final inbreak into history of God's mighty power. They would fight to bring in God's kingdom as "song of light" against all those outside their

---

[1] See S. Schonfeld (ed.) *The Standard Siddur — Prayer Book*, London: J.S.S. Books, 1974.

company who were considered "sons of darkness." The *Pharisees* had a much more pastoral approach than either of these two groups. They genuinely wanted all of God's people to have access to his saving power and to interiorise his kingdom in their everyday lives but they felt that a people who wished to be in touch with the holy God must be totally holy themselves so in practice they too separated themselves off, this time from "sinners," those people in the land who were unable to reach the standard of holiness set down for them. The *Zealots* wished the whole land to be politically the kingdom of God as it had been in the past and so were prepared to use violence to drive the Romans into the sea in order to bring this about.

Jesus inherited the traditions and aspirations of his people in the understanding of God as king but, instead of falling into the trap of exclusiveness or political and religious opportunism like the extreme elements of the parties of his time, he drew afresh on the biblical wellsprings of what the kingdom of God meant. He drew on the concept of God's lordship over his people which, as we have seen, was prominent in the scriptures but he got to the heart of that lordship. It was not to be one of domination but an offer of salvation to everybody. The great saving events which God had effected for his people in the past were now present in the ministry of Jesus himself. In his healings and exorcisms, his kindness and compassion, the reality of God's concern for his people was visible. The kingdom of God, God's special way of dealing with his people, was coming about in the activity of Jesus.

## Kingdom as encounter

The encounters between Jesus and the people of his time, then, showed the kingdom in action. If we go through the gospels we see the ease with which Jesus related to different people in the society of his time. There is a saying of Helder Camara's which could be equally applied to the Jesus from whom he draws his inspiration:

> Let no one be alarmed if I am seen with compromising and dangerous people, of the left or the right, of establishment or opposition, revolutionary or anti-revolutionary, with those of good faith or bad.

Jesus stood out from the cultural environment of his time especially in the way he treated the marginalised: sinners, outcasts, and women. Just as he ate with sinners and touched the outcast leper, so he had no hesitation in engaging in serious conversation with women, even though this was frowned on in the teachings of his people:

> Let no man be alone with any woman in an inn, even with his sister or his daughter or his mother in law, because of public opinion. Let no man chat with a woman in the market place even if she is his wife and, needless to say, with another woman, because of public opinion. Let no man walk behind a woman in the market place even behind his wife and, needless to say, another woman because of public opinion.[2]

---

[2] J. Goldin, *The Fathers According to Rabbi Nathan*, New York: Shocken Books, 1974, p. 17.

It was not customary for a Jewish rabbi to have women disciples and yet many women in the gospels are considered disciples of Jesus. Mary of Bethany, as we have seen, sits at his feet in the attitude of an attentive disciple; Mary Magdalen and the other women *followed* him (a technical term in the gospels for discipleship) even to the cross and beyond (Mk 15:40-16:1). Nowhere has the stereotyping of women been so obvious as in the treatment of Mary Magdalen down the centuries. She has become the symbol of (converted) sexuality and sin and for many this is the only image of women to emerge from the gospels. But if one looks closely at the text, one finds that nowhere is Mary Magdalen associated with being a sinful woman. The confusion arises from identifying the unnamed sinful woman of Luke 7 with Mary Magdalen in Chapter 8 "from whom seven devils had gone out." But there is nothing to indicate that these were sexual devils. In fact elsewhere in the gospels such exorcisms apply to sickness. So it is possible that Mary Magdalen was cured from some kind of psychological illness and as a result was more than grateful to her healer. Nowhere is she seen as anointing Jesus. Mary of Bethany does this in John 12 and more than likely also in Matthew 26 and Mark 14. The woman in Mark anoints Jesus on the head as a symbolic gesture of messianic anointing — a gesture performed in the Old Testament only by priests and prophets (see 1 Sam 10:1; 1 Kings 1:39).

The memory of the different Marys in the life of Jesus got confused early on in the transmission of the stories about his relationships with them and we need to untangle again the richness of the portrait of each individual woman associated with Jesus.

Jesus shows a great sensitivity to women but also a great

sense of reality and plain common sense. One could easily get the impression from other religious writings of the time that women were not part of the world at all or only there as a source of temptation to men. Jesus seems to brush all that aside. He treats women as normal members of society—neither more nor less. They were part and parcel of his bringing in of the kingdom.

It is amazing in a way that so many of these encounters between Jesus and women survived, as very early on the Church seems to have fallen back again into more headline attitudes to women. There is a very funny — if it were not so sad — piece at the end of the *Gospel of Thomas* (a gospel which was rejected as inauthentic even though it has the name of an apostle):

> Simon Peter said to them: "Let Mary leave us, for women are not worthy of life." Jesus said, "I myself shall lead her in order to make her male, so that she too may become a living spirit resembling you males. For every woman who will make herself male will enter the Kingdom of heaven."[3]

This is totally at variance with the attitude of Jesus to women to be found in the four authentic gospels. His attitude must have been too deeply embedded in the tradition to allow such spurious statements to make any headway. Mary Magdalen, after the Resurrection, was shown as the apostle of the apostles; this could not be rejected; hence the attempt to make her male!

Even within the New Testament writings, however, Jesus' attitude could be played down in the light of the socio-political

[3] J. M. Robinson, *The Nag Hammadi Library in English*, Leiden: Brill, 1977, p. 130.

climate of the times (see 1 Tim 2:9-15). There is a great danger in some quarters of the churches today that in assessing Christian attitudes to women, especially in marriage relationships and in Church authority, it is these texts which are used for inspiration rather than the attitude of Jesus himself. Certain elements within the charismatic movement, for instance, have to be criticised for doing this. What has to be done, rather, is to translate the attitude of Jesus into the social environment of our own times.

## Miracles and the kingdom

Many of us were brought up to think of miracles as setting aside the laws of nature and as a proof for the divinity of Christ. But the New Testament does not see miracles in either of these ways; rather they are signs of God's care and compassion present in the encounter between Jesus and human need and human evil. The inbreak of God's kingdom is not in the great might of God's hand shattering the earth (as the image of late Old Testament apocalyptic literature would have it) but in the gentle touch of a man on an elderly woman who was lying in bed sick with a fever (Mk 1:29-31). Neither was it to be in the mighty roar of a God as king scattering his enemies to left and right (see Psalm 2) but in the calm voice of a man saying, "I do will it, be cured" (Mk 1:41).

When the early Church recorded these miracles as inbreaks of God's saving power in the person of Jesus, they were really not too interested in the past event as such but in how it applied to themselves. It is interesting to note that often when

Matthew reports the *healing* of Jesus, Mark, in the exact same incident, speaks of his teaching:

> When he disembarked and saw the vast throng his heart was moved with pity and he *cured* the sick (Mt 14:14);
>
> Upon disembarking Jesus saw a vast throng. He pitied them, for they were like sheep without a shepherd; and he began to *teach* them at great length (Mk 6:34).

The miracles are witness narratives. They are there to encourage an ongoing encounter with God's action in Jesus; healing where healing is needed but, beyond that, enlightenment and repentance, as this modern song of the story of the paralytic brings out:

> Well the commotion occurred in the back of the crowd
> And the noise on the roof got especially loud.
> Out of the ceiling materialised —
> A bed with a person that was paralysed.
> He was completely stiff, rigid, absolutely uptight.
> Well seeing their faith, Jesus asked that one
> What can be your trouble, my son?
> Relax, God loves you despite your sins
> Loosen up a little from the state you're in
> Don't be frightened — you're forgiven
> You're allowed to be freed up some.[4]

We too are encouraged to use the miracles as encounters between ourselves and God. As I pray the scriptures I must ask myself where I need to open myself to God's healing power,

---

[4] R. Beck, *Mark-Rock Gospel*, Parallel Pub. Co. BMI, 1975.

and also where I need to be freed from the perverseness which comes between me and living in the full light of God's love. Only in so far as I do this is the kingdom becoming a reality in my life.

## "The kingdom may be future but the choice is now"

There is a real tension between present and future in the New Testament talk about the kingdom. Those being taught to pray, "Your kingdom come," were those for whom the kingdom was already a matter of personal experience. Why then were they made to speak as if it were future?

The kingdom is the invasion of humanity by God. What is being demanded of the disciples is that the reality which they had already experienced in their lives might grow and continue among them until God's ruling, God's way of looking at things, is complete not only in their own lives but in those of all mankind. Of course this is never a total reality and so the element of future hope and judgment will always be in tension with how far any one person has realised the coming of the kingdom in his or her own life. Like the disciples, we too have experienced God's saving love in our lives but for most of us this is in a very embryonic way. We need continually to pray that more and more we will be tuned into God's wave length and thus in line for bringing in the kingdom.

The word, *come*, is often overlooked in praying the Our Father but it can be made to carry all the weight of this tension between present and future in the realisation of God's kingdom. It can be used to invoke the Spirit groaning for the rebirth of the whole of creation (see Rom 8:22-23) and the longing for the future fulfilment of the kingdom which can be seen in Rev 22:17:

> The Spirit and the Bride say, "Come,"
> Let him who hears answer, "Come."
> Let him who is thirsty come forward;
> Let all who desire it accept the gift of life-giving water.

By repeating, "Your kingdom come," day after day we are asking that God's way of looking at things, God's way of acting, may hold sway more and more in our lives and in the world as a whole. The repetition should be a pledge that we will shoulder our responsibility to try and make this a reality in whatever sphere of influence we may have in life.

There is a Lucan variant to the petition, "Your kingdom come," which says: "May your Holy Spirit come down on us and cleanse us." It is this aspect of the petition which Simone Weil takes up exclusively in her commentary:

> The Kingdom of God means the complete filling of the entire soul of intelligent creatures with the Holy Spirit . . . We can only invite him . . . we must just invite him purely and simply, so that our thought of him is an invitation, a longing cry.[5]

The essence of Jesus' teaching in the Sermon on the Mount is a call to live way beyond what we could possibly do on our own. But we are not on our own, it is the function of the Spirit of God to show us how to live out more and more our initial

---

[5] S. Weil, *Waiting on God*, London: Fontana, 1951, p. 168.

conversion. St. John speaks of him as the one who upbuilds us — this is the meaning of *Paraclete* in the last discourse of John's gospel. He is someone who gets us into shape, keeps us in training so that we will win the fight in the end. St. Catherine of Siena calls the Spirit a "waiter." In her *Dialogue* she makes the Father say of the Spirit: "The Holy Spirit, my loving charity, is the waiter who serves them my gifts and graces." We cannot grasp at the kingdom as one franticly grabs food in an over crowded self-service restaurant. We need the patience to allow ourselves to be waited on; to chew on God's word in prayer and in the rest of our lives, so that we can be assimilated bit by bit to his thoughts, his emotions, his way of seeing things.

## Working for the kingdom

The inner drive of how we work for the kingdom must be in line with that of Jesus but we would not be following his "ability to move beyond the past" if we limited ourselves only to the responses of his time:

> One can never organize the Church's life apart from the Gospels, but one can never organise the totality of the Church's life by making a literal interpretation of the Gospels the limit of all that we should be doing.[6]

As a protest movement within Palestine itself, Christianity was largely a failure but the transfer of the essential message of the inner dynamics of the kingdom to the thought patterns of

[6]*Sign*, Feb. 1980.

the Greco-Roman world eventually transformed that society. Every age has had to think out afresh how to live in the kingdom in its own time. There will always be a tendency to act as a corrective to the age just gone past. So, perhaps, we tend to criticise the past couple of centuries for being too concerned with the good of the individual soul and not enough about the world as such. But it should not be forgotten that it was in these centuries that a great flowering of care and concern for the sick, prisoners and unfortunates of all kinds blossomed in local societies, not to mention the great missionary expansion of the churches. The modern "option for the poor" certainly looks back to the gospel but it also is heir to those who have immediately gone before us.

But, perhaps, in an age threatened by nuclear war we need to go beyond our local groupings also and to think of ourselves as:

> world citizens — leading an ecologically sound life of creative simplicity, sharing our personal wealth with the world's poor and joining with others in the reshaping of institutions in order to bring about a more just global society . . . and in personal renewal through prayer, meditation and study.[7]

These words from a group gathered together from all religions and none are certainly inspired by kingdom attitudes. The kingdom is the opposite to the alienation of structures, of attitudes, of people one from another, in business, in marriage, in society as a whole. Standing in the breach wherever we find these alienating patterns of behaviour can be very painful but

---

[7] From the "Shakertown Pledge," quoted in A.D. Finnerty, *No More Plastic Jesus*, Maryknoll, New York: Orbis Books, 1979, p. 97.

it is often just what is demanded of us if we are to further the action of the kingdom in today's world. We need hearts purified by long prayer to have the true vision of Jesus for our times.

Bringing in the kingdom, therefore, can be a slow, painful process in all our lives. It is only by slow degrees and very imperfectly that we are freed and that we can pass on that freedom so that God's justice and peace can be fulfilled around us. It is only in the kingdom's final fullness that there will be perfect justice. God our Father is always ahead of us, beckoning us on, waiting for us in our future and in that of the world.

## Summary

The kingdom will only come fully with the final coming of Jesus, a kingdom ultimately different to the kingdoms which we build. As Christians we are called to live and think the values of the kingdom before their time has arrived and to make this kingdom a reality even now. Like the Zealots, and even the disciples themselves (see Acts 1:6), we can be content with the expectation of an earthly kingdom. Or we can, like the Sadducees, settle down to the satisfying externals of religion or have the exclusiveness of the Pharisees and Essenes. But Jesus calls us to encounter the saving reality of the kingdom out of our own poverty and emptiness and to bring its message to the poor and alienated of our world. It is only in the power of the Spirit that we can do this.

# 6

# The Good Pleasure of God

> Weep
> If you can,
> Weep,
> But do not complain
> The way choose you —
> And you must be thankful.
>
> *Dag Hammarskjöld*

The sense of urgency in Jesus' saying, "Your kingdom come," is borne out by the next petition, "Your will be done." It is only when God's will is totally fulfilled that the kingdom will have arrived. It would appear from the way the petition is framed that Jesus realised that human beings of themselves are incapable of performing the will of God.

But what exactly do we mean by God's will? It is probably the most misunderstood concept in the whole of religious thinking. How often one has heard, "Blessed be the holy will of God," resignedly spoken in a situation which cried to high heaven for the people involved in it to stand up and do something about the situation themselves. Or it can be used in a very fantastic sense; for example, someone hurt in a car crash may put the accident down to the will of God rather than to the person's own bad driving and feel very aggrieved with God for allowing such a thing to happen. The will of God used in this way can be turned into a sword of Damocles hanging over us to threaten our existence and make life one long series of miseries. Such a misunderstanding makes us think of the will of God as some external force to which we must conform. But that is not how it is; God's will is the truth about life and about ourselves through which we are called to transcend ourselves. The psychologist, Jung, saw this very clearly:

> The belief that God guides us from the centre of our being can completely transform the idea of obedience to God's will. The duty of obeying God has often been conceived of as though it meant submitting to an authority external to us and over against us. Many have revolted against such an obedience because it seemed to belittle their dignity and proper independence. But if the authority to which I submit is within me, then the more I conform myself to its directions the more at one I shall be in myself and the more inner directed.[1]

Jesus was the only perfect example of this:

> In Jesus of Nazareth we have a picture in the vivid colours of a particular human life of the character of the divine pressure which is all the time at work upon us. Jesus Christ presents us with a clue to the nature of the powerful inner force which is ceaselessly urging us to change, to grow to our full stature as human beings, to become what we truly are, to realise our own truth.[1]

[1] C. Bryant, *Jung and the Christian*, London: DLT, 1983, p. 44.

## "Bend my Heart to your will"

The word used for will in the Bible is a word which also means, "good pleasure," "delight." God's gracious will, his delight, is shown in his care for his people and this in spite of the many times they have turned away from him. In the prophet, Isaiah, for example, God, on restoring the people after the Exile, says to them:

> No more shall you be termed, "Forsaken,"
> or your land, "Desolate."
> But you shall be called, "My Delight"
> and your land, "Espoused."
> For the Lord *has his will* in you
> and makes your land his spouse. (Is 62:4)

The background to the understanding of the word, "will," in this passage is the sexual delight of a young man in his bride. When I realised this for the first time it made me do a lot of rethinking about the will of God. I began to realise that what is involved in God's will is really his love for us, a love which is willing to go to any lengths to win us to itself.

The will of God can also be portrayed in terms of a mother's love. Some of the words which are associated with will in New Testament passages are those which are involved with God's "mother love" in the Old Testament. The very familiar hymn, for example, from Ephesians 1 speaks of God's *gracious will* as being God's *choice* of his people in *love* leading them to be children like the *well beloved* one. These are all phrases which appear in the passage from Isaiah 44 which was quoted in Chapter Two in connection with God's mother love (see p. 13).

When the Psalmist therefore asks: "Teach me to do your will for you are my God," he is not really demanding that he be enabled to force his own will in a superhuman effort into conformity with the inscrutable sanctions of a divine tyrant. He is, rather, asking that he, too, may enter into God's pleasure for his people, into an understanding of how God loves us and wants our good. Charles de Foucauld again neatly sums it up in his comment on this petition of the Our Father:

> What in fact are we asking for when we pray that men may do God's will if not that they shall become saints?[2]

It is indicative that in Psalm 119, the great psalm in the Old Testament about doing God's will and conforming to his law, that the Psalmist does not ask: "Bend my *will* to your will, O Lord," but, rather, "Bend my *heart*." In order to understand what the will of God is all about and to enter into it, what we need above all is a change of heart; a change that will enable us to live life from the centre out as it were. This will make us delight in God's way of seeing things rather than being hidebound by our own limited vision of the world.

## "Not my will but Yours . . ."

This turning of the heart is of course where the difficulty lies because we rarely see things from God's point of view. The whole reason for repeating this petition day after day is that we would gradually take on the attitudes of God; his way of

---

[2] de Foucauld, p. 20.

looking at things in the world. It is not a question, therefore, of anxiously scrutinising each action to see if it is "in conformity with the will of God"; rather is it a question of entering into the mindset of God, learning how to look at life from this broader perspective.

There can be no doubt but that there will be difficulty involved. We have only to look at the struggle Jesus himself had to go through. He lived in a turned-away-from-God world and it was a painful process indeed for him to forge a path through it back to God again. He was the only one who fulfilled totally the beautiful ideal of his people which, as we have seen, was at the heart of Jewish prayer in the first century and still is today:

> ... You shall love the Lord, your God, with all your heart, and with all your soul, and with all your strength. (Deut 6:5)

The word for "love" in the Jewish language was a much stronger word than ours. It belonged to the realm of attitudes and behaviour more than to that of feelings. For the Jew, then, to "love" God meant to accept that God *was* God and to act accordingly. To "love with all your heart," meant that one had an undivided and wholehearted approach to God. The rabbis took "with all your soul" to mean, "even if he takes your soul." One must not forsake one's allegiance to God even to escape death. Jesus stood firmly in the Jewish tradition, then, in loving even to the giving of his life. "With all your strength" means with all one's resources since the word translated as "strength" literally means all the heavy things around one. Possessions are not to come between us and God.

Matthew's account of the temptations in the desert takes up these three ways of loving God in Judaism and shows Jesus as a good Jew trying to be totally upright to the Father. Some early Christians took this struggle to be totally upright to God so literally that they ended up leading a life of prayer on top of a pillar. One such stylite (as they were called), when one of his legs went gangrene, cut it off so that he could be even more on a direct line to God standing straight up on one leg on the one pillar.

Jesus did not suffer from such exaggerations but he was totally real about the struggle involved in loving God "with all your heart . . ." This is what is implied in the gospel scene of the Agony in the Garden, as we have seen. The will of God did not come to Jesus there as a heavy sentence imposed from above which he had to endure but as a task which a beloved Son took on in order to accomplish the Father's mission. In John's gospel, the work of the Father is very often equated with doing his will:

> Doing the will of him who sent me and bringing his work to completion is my food.     (Jn 4:34)

The Son did not obey merely in words and acts but in his heart, even if that heart recoiled from the suffering involved. What we must do is to enter with Jesus into this concern for the Father's mission in the world, into his good pleasure that the world be saved. Of course this will involve suffering and of course we will recoil from it but, like Jesus, we must learn to know the face of our God as *Abba* in and through the struggle.

## The gift and the task

The gospels show us the kind of God we are dealing with: one who offers us a new way of living and relating. But they also tell us of the task involved in such living and in such relationships. The deeds (miracles, exorcisms, encounters) of Jesus have been called the *indicative* of God's dealings with human beings. They show how things are — or should be — between God and us. But there is also an *imperative* in the gospels, a call, or rather an invitation, to live out those attitudes in our day to day living:

> The Gospels don't lay down the law. They aren't an assertion: "It's like this and like that." The Gospels are an offer, a naive and diffident offer: "Would you like to live in a completely new way?"[3]

The indicative and the imperative are two parts of the one coin. When one has only the imperative one gets a dry, moralistic religion; where only the indicative, it can taper off into a vague do-goodism.

The teaching of Jesus — the Sermon on the Mount, the parables — enshrine the imperative. The parables call us to risk, to sell everything and buy the field with the treasure in it (Mt 13: 44-46). There is a sense of urgency about many of the parables; the stakes are high and if one dallies on the way it may be too late (Mt 25:1-12). This calls for an ability to travel light (Mt 7:12-27) and to be finely tuned to God's hand (Mt 5:13-16).

---

[3] B. Pasternak, *Doctor Zivago*, London: Fontana, 1958, p. 125.

Failure to understand the parables has more to do with unwillingness than inability (Mk 3:5); what the Old Testament calls "hardness of heart" or, "having a stiff neck." Our age has much experience of the disability caused by hardening of the arteries around the heart and the total disaster it can cause to a person's lifestyle. Suffering periodically from a stiff neck myself makes me aware of the lack of cooperation which is involved by the use of this image. Sometimes one has literally to take one's head in hands and turn it to face the direction needed. Conversion, both initial and ongoing, is often characterised by this symbolic turning around in the Bible. Moses "turns aside" (Ex 3:3) to see the burning bush and his whole life is changed. Mary Magdalen "turns around" at the tomb (Jn 20:14) and has an encounter with the Risen Lord which makes her an apostle to the apostles.

The will of God can never be a stereotyped thing and the living out of it will differ with each person's life. Like Mary, the mother of Jesus, at the Incarnation, we must allow ourselves to be nudged out of the familiar into a totally new way of relating to God. It is the attitude of openness which is all important. It is not incompatible, as in Mary's case, with an attitude of questioning. It is only in prayer and in deep pondering that we can gradually learn to be tuned into the nuances of God's good pleasure for ourselves and for our times. It is not easy for us to see beyond our own prejudices and shortsightedness. There will be many examples of stiff necked decisions in our lives of which we will need to repent. Very often it is not the sins of which we are aware (as individuals or as groups) which most hinder us from entering into God's way of looking at things but those which are embedded in our personalities, even in our race. We need to join in Jesus' loud cry and tears (Heb 5:7) in the effort to carve out in our hearts a way back to the Father. At the same time we should not despair when we make what, by hindsight, can clearly be seen as wrong decisions. We are not thereby out of the will of God for evermore. God can find us anywhere we are in life no matter how we got there, and woo us back to himself again.

## On earth as it is in heaven

Embedded in the scriptures is the realisation that the peace and harmony of the world as a whole is linked to peace and harmony among human beings:

> Kindness and truth shall meet;
> justice and peace shall kiss.
> Truth shall spring out of the earth,
> and justice shall look down from heaven.
> The Lord himself will give his benefits;
> our land shall yield its increase.     (Ps 85:11-13)

We can see the opposite of this peace and harmony in a dramatic way in our own times when we are in danger of blotting out the world entirely in our mad rush to possess more and more.

Doing the will of God "on earth as it is in heaven," then, means bringing the "kindness" and "truth" of God to a world starved for such compassion and fidelity. It means "hungering and thirsting for justice" (Mt 5:6); being brothers and sisters of one another as God is our heavenly Father (see Mt 23:9). It means having a care that God's liberating power finds its right outlet so that true harmony may flourish in the world. Of course this is never a full reality and, as with the saying, "Your kingdom come," so also with, "Your will be done," we are always in tension between the *already* and the *not yet*. Already we may have gone some part of the way towards understanding God's will, God's good pleasure, but we are sadly aware of how little we have really entered into his mind for our world.

## Summary

Jesus' whole life and teaching showed what entering into the Father's good pleasure can involve. It was a life poured out for others. His teaching calls for attitudes of being in the world which seem a reversal of all that we hold dear, but which in reality lead to the living of a more fully human life. As St. Cyprian put it so long ago:

> It was the will of God, then, that Christ both did and taught. It means humility in conduct, steadfastness in faith, modesty in speech, justice in actions, mercy in deeds, discipline in morals; it is to be incapable of doing wrong to anyone and to bear patiently wrong done to us, to keep peace with all and to love God with one's whole heart.[4]

Our tendency is to say, "Let *my* will be done" and to ask God to rubber stamp our plans and ambitions. Following the will of God instead is a calling forth; a call to live beyond ourselves and our own narrow world view.

[4]Quoted in *The Divine Office* III, London: Collins, 1974, p. 202.

# 7

# God Gives Bread

> The Eucharist is the whole of the Bible in substance so that we could have it all in one mouthful.
>
> *Paul Claudel*

What are we asking for when we say: "Give us this day our daily bread"? I suspect that for many of us there is an ambivalence in our thinking and so we do not pray this petition with all the insistency that is implied in it. The earliest commentary on this petition is in the New Testament itself. When in John 6 the crowd say to Jesus, "Sir, give us this bread always," they were thinking of physical bread while the context shows Jesus speaking of himself as the bread of life which is both the wisdom of God (Jn 6:35) and the Eucharist (Jn 6:48). Each of these meanings — physical bread, wisdom/word of God and Eucharist — have been given priority in the understanding of this petition at different times down the ages. Each has a validity of its own in the history of prayer and all three have a place to play at different times in our own life of prayer. It would be well, therefore, to consider each of these interpretations and to see how they can interlock into a coherent whole when we pray: "Give us this day our daily bread."

## God's providential care

Christians are people whom God knows so well that "every hair of your head has been counted" (Mt 10:30) and who, as a result, should not have anxiety in their approach to life's needs. It is interesting to note that the Our Father said at Mass has a prayer for freedom from anxiety inserted between the last petition and the doxology which terminates the prayer in the Liturgy:

> Deliver us, Lord, from every evil and grant us peace in our day. In your mercy keep us free from sin and protect us from all anxiety . . .

Useless anxiety cripples our energies and does not allow them to be free for understanding and following God's ways in the world.

Christians are those who are blessed because they "know their need of God" and as such, "the Kingdom of Heaven is theirs" (Mt 5:3, NEB translation). Being totally poor they are capable of being totally gifted and the kingdom of God's way of looking at things, God's love, can find its way into their hearts and spread through them to others. This was the great insight of St. Thérèse of Lisieux; her way of spiritual childhood was not a question of passivity, waiting around for God to do everything. She used her human capacity to love to the fullest but at the same time she laid claim to the totality of God's love with a child's capacity to take for itself everything offered to it. At the same time she had a heart "stern as death" (Cant 8:6) to suffer and to do all that was necessary to pass on that love.

Some Christians will be literally called on to live on Providence as an example of this love for the rest of us. I know of an Evangelical community on the West Bank in Israel, for example, who pray in every penny they need to run an orphanage and school for young Arab children. Of course this does not mean that we can sit back and do nothing about providing for our needs. The Our Father is the perfect grace before meals because in it children can recognise that it is through the work of their parents that the food is placed on the table day after day. I once heard of a family whose father had died but the results of whose work was still putting food on the table long after his death. The Our Father said at each meal became a way of remembering their father and thanking God for him.

## "Bread is life to the destitute . . ." (Sirach 34:21)

This petition of the Our Father is not an insurance policy, however, taken out on God, forcing him to provide for all our needs. It too enters into the doing of God's will. It is God's good pleasure that his people be fed, be made whole, but so many of us thwart that good pleasure by grabbing more than our share, by making the satisfaction of our own needs the total horizon of our world. Inherent in this petition, therefore, is a sense of obligation to provide for the needs of others. We ask in the plural, after all: "Give *us* this day our daily bread."

> What good is it to profess faith without practicing it? Such faith has no power to save one, has it? If a brother or sister has nothing to wear and no food for the day, and you say to them, "Good-bye and good luck! Keep warm and well fed," but do not meet their bodily needs, what good is that? So it is with the faith that does nothing in practice. It is thoroughly lifeless" (Jas 2:14-17).

The passage from Sirach which heads this section goes on to say: "And it is murder to deprive them of it." "Can there be an *Abba*-experience without a struggle against Mammon?" asks a recent writer in *Concilium*. Today we realise more and more that we are not merely asked to give bits of bread to the poor. It could mean to a Christian politician in the West, for example, that he not stand idly by and watch multinationals rob developing countries of the very grain genes which are at the basis of all food production and then cynically sell them their own packaged products. It will certainly mean in all parts of the world that many Christians will be called to political activism to try and alleviate the oppressive structures which weigh on the poor, even in the best of our societies. For all of us it will mean acting, not out of enlightened self-interest, but with a heart open to love our neighbour as ourselves, whatever that may demand of us in the concrete situation. It will certainly demand that we treat the least in our communities with respect and ackowledge their dignity. The Little Brothers and Sisters, followers of Charles de Foucauld, once again can be guidelines to us on how to do this:

The witness of friendship is already a path to evangelisation and a ferment of liberation; for simply looking with love and sensitivity at a poor person provokes a liberating interior transformation and contains a manifestation of God's love. And, besides, this loving look given to someone poor is a testimony to others, for it reveals the greatness and the dignity of those who are considered poor and little.[1]

## "Not on bread alone ... but on every Word"

The physical reality does not exhaust the meaning of bread as it is used in the gospels. Jesus is of course shown partaking of food like any normal human being. He could enjoy feasts and weddings like any one of us, yet there were times when he had "no time even to eat" (Mk 6:30-31), because of the demands of his mission. He pointed beyond the physical reality of bread continually. One can see this, for example, in the way the miracle of the loaves and fish is reported in the gospels. I do not agree with the interpretation which says that all that was involved was that Jesus' words loosened people's pockets, as it were, and those who had bread hidden under their cloaks produced it and shared it with the rest present. I think Rosemary Haughton gets nearer to the reality when she points out that the miracle was wrung out of Jesus as part of the ongoing understanding of his mission which was opening up before him:

---

[1] Little Brothers and Little Sisters of Jesus, *Cry the Gospel with your Life*, Denville, New Jersey: Dimension Books, pp. 203-204.

The people were hungry, they needed food and it seems possible, indeed likely that the challenge of it had been growing in the back of his mind while he was teaching and healing them. These people, out there in the "wilderness" were so obviously just like their ancestors dependent on the Lord's bounty, ignorant and bewildered yet hopeful. If he did not send them away to get food before they reached the point at which they ran the risk of "fainting on the way," it could have been because the sight of them and its associations (with the manna, and with the hopes of the "messianic banquet") were driving him imaginatively towards the action he in fact took.[2]

The satisfying of physical hunger came first but beyond that came the whole understanding of the reality of the action of God's word for his people in the past, that word which Jesus was now fulfilling in himself.

In the Old Testament the Word of God was often symbolised by the imagery of food:

> Why spend your money for what is not bread;
> Your wages for what fails to satisfy?
> Heed me, and you shall eat well ...
> You shall delight in rich fare.     (Is 55:2)

The early Christian writers often spoke of the Word of God, both in the Old and the New Testament, as food to be chewed on, ruminated overmuch as a cow chews the cud. The following rather crude image from St. Caesarius of Arles shows how this daily chewing can enable us to pass on the Word of God to others almost unbeknownest to ourselves, that is, if we have assimilated it well first:

---

[2] R. Haughton, *The Passionate God*, London: DLT, 1981, p. 77.

For as the cows wander through the fields and the meadows and go through vineyards and olive groves and from the leaves and grass they graze on provide milk for the calves; so ministers assiduously reading the Word of God on the wide hills of the Scriptures, should from the herbiage they gather, provide spiritual milk for their children.[3]

This breaking of the Word of God for others is not only done by "ministers." Many of us can bear witness to the power of the word released in a group setting, be it in study or in prayer or in reviewing life together around the scriptures. This releasing of the word for a group is a real function of prophecy in today's world. When a community group is together around the the Word of God, it is the person with the gift of prophecy who is able to grasp the meaning of this particular passage for the community and convey that to the others present in contemporary terms so that they can be encouraged, built up and strengthened.

"Give us this day our daily bread," then, can be said as a prayer for the assimilation of our daily dose of the Word of God, whether in the Liturgy, together with others in a community setting, or in our own private prayer. It can gradually transform our emotions, our actions and our thoughts until we take on God's way of looking at things, God's way of acting in the world.

---

[3]Quoted in M.F. Toal (ed) *The Sunday Sermons of the Great Fathers II*.

## "I am the living bread"

The table of the Word is complemented by the table of the Eucharist in the Liturgy. The "heart burning within" at the opening of the scriptures often only recognises Jesus at the "breaking of the bread," as happened to the disciples on the road to Emmaus (Lk 24:13-35). Right down the centuries this petition of the Our Father was seen as a cry for the Eucharist. St. Teresa of Avila, for instance, in her quaint commentary on the Our Father says:

> For the love of God let us realise the meaning of our good Master's petition. We know that until the accidents of bread have been consumed by our natural heat, the good Jesus is with us. If, while he went about in the world, the sick were healed by merely touching his clothes, how can we doubt that he will work miracles when he is within us; if we have faith?[+]

It is felt that this is more than ordinary bread we are talking about in this petition; it is the bread of the messianic banquet we are asking for, when the Father himself will feed his own in the ingathering of the peoples (see Ex 16:4). Table fellowship with Jesus was a sign of that ingathering (Lk 22:29-30). We now share in that table fellowship. There is again a real tension between the present and the future just as there was in earlier petitions. One modern commentator translates the petition as: "The bread for tomorrow, give us today." In the Liturgy of the Eucharist we celebrate the "not yet" as if it "already were" in order to "bring it about" — the "not yet" of our union with

[+]Translation by the Carmelites, Newry, Co. Down.

God and with one another, as if it "already were" since we know that this union is far from being a reality among us. But we can at least present our bodies in a physical presence with our brothers and sisters and before our common Father "in order to bring it about." In eating the bread of life day after day we can be gradually changed to "put on the mind of Christ" (see Phil 2:1-11) as we face our daily tasks and commitments:

> Jesus gives to the children of God the privilege of stretching out their hands to grasp the glory of the consummation, to fetch it down, believe it down, to pray it down — right down into their poor lives, now already, here already, this day already.[5]

## "As bread that is broken"

But by praying in this way we implicitly lay ourselves open to the possibility of brokenness which was the lot of Jesus himself. This brokenness draws together the three ways we have considered of understanding the petition, as the following quotation from the *Teaching of the Twelve Apostles* brings out:

> As this broken bread was scattered over the hills
> and then when gathered became one mass
> so may your Church be gathered
> from the ends of the earth into your kingdom.

The early Christian martyrs used the image of the broken bread to show the white heat of their own love for God, as this example from St. Ignatius of Antioch demonstrates:

---

[5] J. Jeremias, *Expository Times* 71 (1959/1960) 145.

> For my part, I am writing to all the Churches and assuring them that I am truly in earnest about dying for God — if only you yourselves put no obstacle in the way. I must implore you to do me no such untimely kindness. I ask you to allow me to become a meal for the beasts, for it is they who provide my way to God; I am his wheat; ground fine by the lion's teeth to be made purest bread for Christ. So interceed with him for me, that by their instrumentality I may be made a sacrifice to God.[6]

Serving God in the poor and destitute today have brought many to the same fate. As Pope John Paul said about probably the most famous of modern day martyrs:

> Archbishop Romero, that zealous pastor was murdered ... when he ws celebrating holy Mass. He crowned his ministry, devoted particularly to the poorest and most marginalised, with his blood. It was a supreme witness which has become a symbol of the tribulations of a whole people but also a motive of hope for a better future.[7]

We will not all be asked to lay down our lives in a violent fashion but we have all to be prepared to participate in the brokenness of the body of Christ if we are to be his followers. When saying, "Give us this day our daily bread," then, especially at the Eucharist, we are crying with all God's people: Help us to understand and live the reality of bread, the brokenness of bread, so that we can live to the full the joy of the Resurrection.

---

[6]Quoted in *The Divine Office III*, London: Collins, 1974, p 338.

[7]Quoted in F. Dussel, "The Bread of the Eucharistic Celebration as a Sign of Justice in the Community," *Concilium* 152 (1982) 56.

## Summary

There is a real interdependence between the three ways of understanding this petition. What we celebrate in the Eucharist is ultimately God's gift of life to us and the demand that we share that life with others. In the scriptural accounts of Jesus as the Word of God we have the supreme example of that sharing.

# 8

# God Forgives

Forgive us our Father for we have sinned against you;
Wipe away our transgressions from before your eyes . . .
Look upon our afflictions and strive in our striving;
Redeem us for your name's sake.

This passage from the Jewish liturgy shows how strong the realisation of the need for forgiveness was in the tradition from which Jesus came. There is a strong sense of sin in the Old Testament but the understanding of it is different from our way of looking at sin. Instead of being considered as "any wilful thought, word, deed or omission contrary to the law of God" (as an old catechism definition had it), sin was looked on as a failure to live out a relationship. There is no one single word for sin in the Bible; instead words which have meanings like "miss the mark," "take a short cut," "rebellion," "folly" were used in connection with the action of breaking off a relationship with God and with one's fellow human beings.

Adam and Eve are shown as being tempted to take a short cut to knowledge, a knowledge which when they possessed it only caused them shame and hardship (Gen 3); Saul failed to live up to his obligations as king and so found himself bypassed for David. Sin is often described as infidelity or even adultery, a betrayal of a deep relationship with God (see Ezek 16). God, however, is always ready to receive back the erring one and from this stems the reality of forgiveness. Already in the Old Testament, as we have seen, forgiveness was linked with the image of God as father. The characteristic of compassion and forgiveness is actually a feminine quality as Pope John Paul's encyclical, *Rich in Mercy*, points out:

> From the deep and original bond — indeed the unity — that links a mother to her child there springs a particular love. Of this love one can say that it is completely gratuitous, not merited and that in this aspect it constitutes an interior necessity, an exigency of the heart ... (The word for mercy) generates a whole range of feelings; including goodness and tenderness, patience and understanding that is, readiness to forgive.

In the light of this insight into forgiveness, it seems something of an anomaly that the Church in past centuries did not harness women's particular gifts in the exercise of the ministry of reconciliation and forgiveness. Nor does the encyclical go on to suggest that a change should be made now. Women have, in spite of that, often exercised their special gifts of sensitivity and compassion to portray God's forgiveness to his people but outside the ministerial areas. Surely the time has come to change all that.

## Jesus and forgiveness

The forgiveness of sins for those who remained faithful to God was to be one of the chief blessings of the Messianic times so eagerly awaited at the time of Jesus:

> And there shall be forgiveness of sins
> And every mercy and peace and forbearance. (1 Enoch 5:6)

Jesus brought that forgiveness especially to those who were not able to know, let alone keep, the whole weight of tradition and law enjoined on them by the religious leaders of the time. The most lenient of these leaders, the great Rabbi Hillel, is supposed to have said that an ignorant person could not be saintly; it was felt that deep study of the law was necessary to become holy. Because they were not able to study many felt guilty and left out of salvation. This kind of guilt can be a terrible bind on people; it can extend to a kind of magical imposition of religious acts on oneself or on others which, if they cannot be complied with, makes the person feel totally lost. There is the example of the child giving up sweets for Lent and not being able to resist one on a particular day; this led her to expect God to knock her off her bicycle the next time she went for a ride. We should be courageous in getting rid of anything that binds us in a superstitious way and most of us have our own particular fetish.

Jesus, in the passage:

> Come to me all you who are weary and find life burdensome, and I will refresh you. (Mt 11:28)

gave hope to the little people of his time who were too busy to keep the minutiae of the traditional interpretation of the law which was being demanded of them. By freeing them from the burdens on their backs, he enabled them to look up again and see what kind of God they were to meet.

The famous parable of the prodigal son (Lk 15:11-32), now increasingly called the "prodigal father" (as Wilfrid Harrington's book in this series points out) shows the nature of God as a father who is prodigal of forgiveness. The forgiveness shown in the parable borders on indulgence; we would agree that it was quite in order for the father to accept back his erring son but surely a good sound talking-to would be a better sequel than throwing a party for *his* friends (v. 29), the very ones who had probably led him astray in the first place. The characteristics of the picture of God shown here are again more feminine than masculine. In reality it is much more often the mother who looks anxiously down the road every day to see if the erring one is on the horizon and then, when he does come, shields him from the father's wrath and disappointment.

Be that as it may, there is a totality about the love shown that we, along with the elder brother, find very hard to accept but which we must do if we are to draw down God's forgiveness on ourselves. As has often been pointed out, this is the one petition in the Our Father which has a condition attached. Jesus was insistent that forgiveness of one another was essential if we are to learn how to relate to God. Even though there is no record of the Our Father in Mark's gospel, in it the call to forgive is closely linked with prayer:

> When you stand to pray, forgive anyone against whom you have a grievance so that your heavenly Father may in turn forgive you your faults. (Mk 11:25)

In Matthew's Sermon on the Mount there is the same kind of insistence: we must be reconciled to one another before offering our gift at the altar (Mt. 5:23). Indeed this petition is the only one in the Our Father on which Matthew offers a comment:

> If you forgive the faults of others, your heavenly Father will forgive you yours. If you do not forgive others, neither will your Father forgive you. (Mt 6:14-15)

It could not be more pointed. It is not a question here of bargaining with God but of taking on his attitudes and ways of acting which, as we have seen, include forgiveness. Genuine communion with God brings a new understanding of our relationships with one another.

## Forgiveness and resentment

Forgiveness is so little part of our nature that most of us are hardly aware of the deep resentments which cloud our vision and sour our taste for reality. One of the great fruits of modern psychology is the realisation of the unconscious, the depths of myself of which I am almost totally unaware but which deeply influence my attitudes and behavior. What most clogs us and trips us up is not the obvious resentments but those which are deep down and have become so much a part of us that we are not even aware of their presence.

I remember once being part of a group sharing on the need for forgiveness in our lives. Each person there spoke of the need to forgive father or mother, spouse or friend who had wounded him or her deeply in life. I did not share because I could not honestly at that moment consciously think of anyone who had hurt me that deeply. Afterwards in prayer I realised that even if I had not much in the way of personal hurts to cope with, deep within my bones were the resentments of oppression and misunderstandings between the families and clans of my background, where resentment over land can be very deepseated. Then there was the whole area of oppression between my nation and England on which I had been fed as a child. I realised that this and much besides had to be forgiven if I were really to be a vehicle for the forgiveness of God in my relations with others. It is only in the measure that we ourselves let go of our resentments and learn to truly forgive that true peace and justice can be built up between persons, between families and nations.

## Intercession

We are not alone in the effort and anguish that real forgiveness involves. As in the Jewish prayer quoted at the beginning of this chapter, we ask God to "strive in our strivings." This leads naturally to intercession since, just as the Father does not abandon the prodigal son he has forgiven, so neither can we merely forgive and forget. One of the hardest things I know is to carry the person who has injured one before the Lord in prayer and to ask for that person's good in deep sincerity. But one of the first examples of intercession recorded in the Bible is precisely that: Abraham asked to pray for healing for the man who had taken away his wife, Sarah (Gen 20:17). The rabbis say of this episode that when Abraham prayed a knot was untied, that is the tangled relationship between man and God was straightened out and from then on it was possible to pray. Intercession is all about untying knots and many situations in the world today, where forgiveness of one nation by another seems impossible, demand that we bring them before the Lord in mute prayer begging that knots will be untied.

In the prayer of forgiveness and intercession we release one another and give back life. But of course this has to be followed up by the appropriate physical action in the relationship. We will never fully realise how totally dependent we are on one another for the freeing word of forgiveness but also for the carrying of one another's burdens which it implies.

Simone Weil brings out another aspect of this petition in her commentary on the Our Father. She takes the translation, "debts" for transgressions literally (and it is the more original):

> At the moment of saying these words we must have already remitted everything that is owing to us. This not only includes reparation for any wrongs we think we have suffered but also gratitude for the good we think we have done, and it applies in a quite general way to all we expect from people and things, to all we consider our due and without which we should feel ourselves to have been frustrated.[1]

Even if we forgive obvious hurts we still cling to such debts: resentment that life has not given due recognition to our merits, resentment for the arthritic pain which has come because of the dampness of our place of work; resentment that husband, wife, child has not appreciated us fully; that life has given us a raw deal . . . the list is endless.

[1] S. Weil, pp. 172, 173.

As Simone Weil goes on to say, this type of resentment comes chiefly from the imagination that we are permanent and that all life centers around us:

> From our point of view the equilibrium of the world is a combination of circumstances so ordered that our personality remains intact and seems to belong to us. All the circumstances of the past which have wounded our personality appear to us to be disturbances of balance which should infallibly be made up for one day or another by phenomena having a contrary effect. We live on the expectation of these compensations. The near approach of death is horrible chiefly because it forces the knowledge upon us that these compensations will never come.[2]

This is the deepest poverty, the greatest letting-go. We need above all to forgive ourselves, to let go of resentment against life itself, even against God. We need to bring each day in prayer before the Lord what in us needs to be healed, made whole by forgiveness. It is only by forgiving such debts in total poverty and in accepting God's forgiveness for our blind clinging to them in the past that we can come to know the true meaning of life and of his love.

## Summary

Accepting our need of forgiveness is a basic human insight. We realise in our best moments that we are turned away from God and from our fellow human beings, locked up in ourselves and in our own dishonesty. Most of the time, however,

---

[2] S. Weil, p. 174.

we are not even aware of our blindness and so we need the prayer of Jesus in Luke:

> Father, forgive them; they do not know what they are doing.
> (Lk 23:34)

Forgiven ourselves, we can then forgive others and we must do so if we are to be truly on the road to God.

# 9

# God and Evil

No one can obtain the kingdom of heaven
who has not passed through temptation.

*A saying attributed to Jesus*

Some see a direct link between the last petition of the Our Father and the one immediately before it so that both together can be translated as:

> Forgive us our debts and — so that we may not incur new debts of sin — let us not be led into temptation but snatch us away from evil.[1]

Our greatest temptation is the desire to be left alone with only our own resources to face the onslaught of evil. It is the temptation to "go it alone" to feel that we are sufficient to

---

[1] Petuchowski, p. 101.

ourselves. But experience shows us often how wrong we are; how much we are in need of support. The essence of this petition, then, is a cry for liberation, liberation from the evil within as much as from that all around us. If we recognise temptation for what it is, this cry is automatically forced out of us in much the same way as a cry for help is forced out of a drowning man.

There are many passages in the Bible, as we have seen, which speak of God having to answer a cry for help when the people as a whole or individuals are in dire straits. God is expected to hear the cry of the poor against their oppressors (Ex 22:22) and the cry of someone unjustly accused (Dan 13:42). Temptation is just such a deadly peril and God will be expected to listen to the cry of those who are in such distress.

We are asking to be spared from temptation, not to be allowed to face it because we know that we will not have the strength to do so. This seems to be the meaning of Jesus' injunction to the disciples in the Garden to pray that they might not be led into temptation (Mt 26:41). In the echo of this scene in John's gospel, this would seem to be Jesus' own prayer for himself: "Father, save me from this hour" (Jn 12:27). Some commentators, however, would translate this as "save me *throughout* this hour." The temptation, the great trial, has to be, but Jesus is not alone and neither are we; the Father is there "throughout."

On the cross, however, Jesus seemed totally delivered up to evil, abandoned by the Father: "My God, my God why have you forsaken me" (Mt 27:46). This cry has been interpreted in this century as a cry of despair on the part of Jesus, but scholars are more inclined to see it as Matthew's presentation of the biblical picture of the just person seemingly abandoned by God but keeping his trust in God in spite of all appearances to the contrary and in this way being saved throughout the trial. For Matthew, the crucifixion is the completion of the earlier temptation scene where Jesus had rejected the temptation to be his own man, to live from himself. Instead he would, as we have seen, "Love the Lord with all his heart . . ." The cry of the Satan in the temptation scene (Mt 4:3,6) is taken up by the mockers at the cross: "If you are God's Son . . ." (Mt 27:40). But Jesus proves he is the Son of God not by giving in to the temptation to come down from the cross, but by showing his commitment to love God and mankind "with all his heart . . ." to the end. We, too, are called to remain faithful within temptation and trial, to love God and others right to the end. A way of translating this petition of the Our Father could therefore be: "Dissolve our fear, release us for trust."

## Everyday temptation or end time temptation?

What exactly is meant by temptation in this petition? Many opt for the everyday temptations which life brings our way, while others see in question here the great trial of the end times. But it does not have to be an either-or situation. Every facing of temptation is a fight against evil. We are always living in the end times and the Church is always engaged in the great struggle to show the true face of God within a world which is determined to shut it out. The struggle goes on in its own ranks as much as outside. Today our ordinary lives are drawing us more and more into the arena of that struggle. Maybe one is a religious in Central America, in constant danger of prison or death for standing on gospel principles, or a young married couple in the West faced with the prospect of job loss for insisting on the same principles. Even if in less dramatic ways, all of us are called to take our part in the struggle.

If we are to grow we have to embrace that struggle. The temptation not to "love the Lord with all our heart" is as real for us as for Jesus in the desert. We can allow the hunger and thirst and the comforts of life to come between us and the going out of ourselves in love to God and to others. Most of the temptations in life are temptations to take short cuts, to take the easy way out. They are always tailored to our own particular vocation in life and our own temperament. Maybe a young mother is tempted not to listen to a child's cry in the night when she is very tired or someone preaching the Word of God skimps on the necessary homework. Our vision is being dulled the whole time by the day in, day out temptations we give in to, so that we are not clear enough in mind or heart when the bigger ones come our way.

More and more today Christians feel that they cannot survive the struggle on their own and our times have seen a phenomenal increase in support groups of all kinds. This petition is also in the plural after all. Reviewing life together in the light of God's Word can be a great source of strength and an impetus to live at a deeper level. The only danger can be where leadership in the group becomes over authoritarian, usually among the men. One then ends up in a new type of patriarchal society. The temptation is always there not to make the effort for ourselves, to abdicate our responsibility and take the easy way out by merely obeying rules and regulations laid down for us.

The possibilities of deceiving ourselves by what appears to

be the good are endless — as Paul learnt in dealing with the bunch of converts he had made at Corinth. His first epistle to the Corinthians shows how a close knit community can provide a counter environment to the evil all around but it also shows the pitfalls which can endanger relationships within and without the group. The New Testament as a whole gives a very realistic assessment of the nature of the struggle in which we are engaged but it also reiterates that we are not alone in that struggle (see Jn 8:16). The rather bizarre imagery of the Book of Revelation has no other purpose than to bring home to the first Christians, in the thought patterns and language with which they were familiar from late Old Testament times, that the same God who had been with his people in past trials and tribulations would be with them also in present ones. With this assurance the early Christians were enabled to face life with great courage and boldness, a courage which can be ours for the asking:

> Now, Lord, consider their threats and enable your servants to speak your word with great boldness. Stretch out your hand to heal and perform miraculous signs and wonders through the name of your holy servant Jesus.(Acts 4:29-30; New International Bible version)

This courage and boldness which is not of ourselves, marks the true disciples of Jesus.

## God and evil

Thought of temptation inevitably leads to the question of evil which in turn leads to wonderment as to how God can allow evil. How often people's belief in God is shattered because of the death, for example, of an innocent child. This was a major problem also for the later books of the Old Testament, in particular for the book of Job. We are so used to invoking the "patience of Job" that it comes as quite a shock when we read the book to find that he was the most impatient of human beings. True, the first few chapters, the Prologue of the book, give us the traditional image: a rich desert sheikh who has fallen on evil times but who takes his downfall with good grace. The end of the book, some forty chapters later, shows Job restored to God's favour and given back "double of what he had before."

Chrisitan writers down the ages, remembering St. James' admiration of Job's patience (Jas 5:11), have largely concentrated on these two sections of the book, leaving out of account the forty chapters in between from which a very different picture of Job emerges; instead of patient suffering and humble acceptance of God's will, we get a violent attack on the Almighty and anguished questionings of his wisdom and justice in the government of the universe and of his dealings with human beings — particularly with those who were suffering unjustly as Job believed himself to be.

It was part of the tradition of his people that God and they were partners in a covenant which bound them to "fear God and turn away from evil" (Job 1:1). On God's part it was felt that he would reward those who complied and punish those who did not. The friends who came to comfort Job trotted out this traditional answer. For them it was all very simple: Job was suffering; therefore he must have done something deserving of such punishment. But Job himself was as much convinced of his innocence as he was aware of his suffering and, spurred on by the insensitivity of the friends, he rails against the God whom he believes to be the author of this injustice. Job's world had collapsed about his ears; he was in a state very familiar to us from modern existentialist writers:

> A world that can be explained by reason however faulty is after all a familiar world. But in a universe that has suddenly been deprived of illusions and light, man feels a stranger because he is deprived of memories of a lost homeland to the same degree that he lacks the hope of a promised land to come.[2]

The problem of the suffering of the innocent in the book of Job, therefore, is subsumed into the deeper problem of our relations with God. Job hovers between the God he sees as Destroyer and God as Vindicator:

> But as for me, I know that my Vindicator lives,
> and that he will at last stand forth upon the dust;
> whom I myself shall see;
> my own eyes, not another's shall behold him,
> and from my flesh I shall see God.  (Job 19:25-27)

Some have been a direct reference to the Resurrection in these lines. If they were, Job's problem would have been solved since he could feel that his sufferings would be rewarded in the after-life. But this is often too facile a solution and allows people not to solve problems in this life because they feel they will all be solved hereafter. Marx was right to condemn such "pie in the sky" religion. For Job, at any rate, this was no

---

[2] A Camus, *Le Myth de Sisyphe*, quoted in D. Cox, *The Triumph of Impotence*, Rome: Gregorian University Press, 1978, p. 32.

solution since in his time the after-life was only considered as a shadowy kind of existence in Sheol where one could no longer know anything — least of all God.

In Job's eventual encounter with God he does not receive any answers to the problem of suffering but he deepens immeasurably his understanding of God. The grandeur of Job is that:

> having found that the absolute supplies no answers, Job carries on both his fidelity to that absolute and his striving after the unknowable.[3]

It is an attitude which will ring true for many today for whom the absence of God is a much more real experience than his presence. For Job, in spite of all his doubts and railings against God, is commended for his fidelity rather than the friends:

> For you have not spoken rightly concerning me, as has my servant Job. (Job 42:8)

The answer to the problem of innocent suffering is largely left unanswered in the book of Job, then, but by its questionings this book more than any other in the Old Testament opened the way towards the solution which Jesus had to offer. The gospels do not answer the problem any better than the book of Job but what they do is to show us that when a Christian meets God, it is no longer a God speaking "out of the whirlwind" in power and majesty (Job 38:1) but one who, though innocent, entered into human suffering at its depths. This has given a whole new dimension to human suffering as Teilhard de Chardin was quick to see:

---

[3] D. Cox, p. 172.

Human suffering, the sum total of suffering poured out at each moment over the whole earth, is like an immeasurable ocean. But what makes up this immensity? Is it blackness, emptiness, barren wastes? No, indeed; it is potential energy. Suffering holds hidden within it, in extreme intensity the ascensional force of the world. The whole point is to set this force free by making it conscious of what it signifies and of what it is capable. For if all the sick people in the world were simultaneously to turn their sufferings into a single shared longing for the speedy completion of the kingdom of God through the conquering and organising of the earth, what a vast leap towards God the world would thereby make.[4]

## Summary

The last petition of the Our Father, then, is not one that asks to sidestep the sufferings of life. It is a great cry from the heart of Christians that we will not succumb to the powers of evil under temptation and go over to their side. Rather, that we will have a clear vision to see what is really of evil in our world and in ourselves. Then we can take our stand with Jesus firmly in God's camp and go through with the sufferings involved in the living out of a christian life to the end.

---

[4]P. Teilhard de Chardin, *Hymn of the Universe*, London: Collins, 1977, pp. 85-86.

# 10

# Into Your Hands

> You must be made perfect as your
> heavenly Father is perfect.
>
> Mt 5:48

By his use of the model of fatherhood for God, rather than of any other model, Jesus laid stress on the fact that we must become like God; we must grow up to be formed into the likeness of the one in whose image we are made (Gen 1:26-27). What does it mean to be made in the "image" of God? Later books of the Bible meditated on and worked over the statement of Genesis and saw it as giving us a capacity to act like God in the world: creatively and with power over the rest of creation (see Sirach 17:1-13). But not everyone makes use of the capacity to act like God. Jesus was the only one to do so fully and, in so far as we follow him, we too can enter more and more into God's likeness.

This is what Matthew means by being "made perfect as your heavenly Father is perfect." It is a phrase which has caused a lot of misunderstanding down the centuries; it does not mean having a perfectionist mentality which is always striving to tie up loose ends and have everything in order. Jesus' mode of life would have driven a perfectionist crazy; maybe that was why Judas could take it no more. Neither does it involve a computer-like attitude to the keeping of laws where we tot up all our scores and expect God to reward us for our goodness. In the Old Testament the Israelites were called to "be holy for I, the Lord your God, am holy" (Lv 19:2). Jesus read the same Torah as the Pharisees but they translated this into a tight system of obedience to strict ritual law, while Jesus threw it wide open to reveal the heart of God.

The word Matthew uses could be better translated as "whole" or "complete" rather than as "perfect": we are to act so as to be whole or complete like God. The context shows what Matthew meant by that "wholeness" or "completeness":

> You have heard the commandment, 'you shall love your countryman but hate your enemy.' My command to you is: love your enemies, pray for your persecutors. This will prove that you are sons of your heavenly Father, for his sun rises on the bad and the good, he rains on the just and the unjust. (Mt 5:43-45)

This is a very good example of the necessity of not quoting a gospel text in isolation from its context. Being "perfect" is not an abstract definition for Matthew. He shows us very concretely in what God's perfection consists which we are to imitate. When we have the same ability as God to love indiscriminately then, and only then, are we whole people. And it is not a question of loving in a general kind of way. We are called to love the people who might be our enemies and who are actually persecutors. Anyone who has been in such a situation knows how difficult that is; the bombing and destruction which is still going on even in the name of Christianity shows how little we have taken this passage to heart. It is only when we do so that we can show forth the family likeness to God; that we are sons and daughters of a Father who loves with an all embracing love, brothers and sisters of him who said:

> Father, forgive them; they do not know what they are doing. (Lk 23:35)

Luke, when he is transmitting the saying we are considering, does not say "you must be made perfect . . ." but, "Be compassionate, as your Father is compassionate" (Lk 6:36). The context is again that of loving enemies. We are asked to show compassion to those who have done us wrong. We are to show care and concern not just for those we love but even to those whom we feel have let us down. Jesus' whole life was an understanding of this great magnanimity of God and passing it on to us. This is what St. John means when he says:

> I solemnly assure you,
> the Son cannot do anything by himself
> he can do only what he sees the Father doing.
> For whatever the Father does,
> the Son does likewise.
> For the Father loves the Son
> and everything the Father does he shows him. (Jn 5:19-20)

## Praying the Our Father

The Our Father, then, is Jesus' communication to us of his own great longing that the Father's likeness would be more and more imprinted on us. He longed that the kingdom, God's way of acting in the world, would be a reality in the lives of his disciples. He taught them that in order to bring this about they must open themselves up to allow God's good will, God's good pleasure, work itself out in their lives. He begged them to pray for the strength to do this in the cry for bread, bread for life and bread of life. They were to take on God's attitudes of forgiveness and to trust for the protection of his name in the time of evil.

In our life of prayer, then, the Our Father can transform us more and more into the likeness of our God. It can be the ache of our heart to grow more and more into the heart of God. There is an old Irish poem which speaks of love as a "grief lodged under the skin, strength pushed beyond its bounds." As we pray the Our Father day after day, it can become such a "grief" urging us to become more like God in our lives; a "strength" which pushes us "beyond bounds" in the effort to makes us grow up to be like our God. It is only then that we will have the wholeness to take on the attitudes which Jesus revealed to us as being the attitudes of his God.

One of Teilhard de Chardin's other great insights was the realisation that the God who was *up above* was also *on ahead*. As a young girl, living under the shadow of the beautiful Killarney mountains of my native county gave me a great sense of the Beyond in life, a Beyond which very often since has become more like one of those will o' the wisps in the bogs of that same county.

God is a reality who is always pulling me beyond where I am now; beyond the many businesses I am engaged in, even those which are for religion's sake; someone who "surprises me by joy," to use C. S. Lewis' phrase, or knocks me over with unfounded melancholy even in the midst of joy. Someone too who at this particular point of time is calling me to take seriously the full womanhood that for too long I have ignored, not in an aggressive way but conscious of how much the feminine side of us has to offer to our world and to an understanding of God.

When all is said and done, however, I feel that *Abba* still expresses best for me the reality of this God and the Our Father is the prayer that more and more brings me into relationship with that *Abba*. Calling God, "Father," then makes me realise that ultimately I have no control over either my birth or my death. My life is a gift and I must realise that I am a dependent being, dependent for life but also in death, a death which is not at the mercy of blind fate but into the hands of one who is called *Abba*.